Sequencing?

Sequencing?
Financial Strategies for Developing Countries

Alison Harwood and Bruce L. R. Smith, Editors

BROOKINGS INSTITUTION PRESS
Washington, D.C.

About Brookings

The Brookings Institution is a private nonprofit organization devoted to research, education, and publication on important issues of domestic and foreign policy. Its principal purpose is to bring knowledge to bear on current and emerging policy problems. The Institution was founded on December 8, 1927, to merge the activities of the Institute for Government Research, founded in 1916, the Institute of Economics, founded in 1922, and the Robert Brookings Graduate School of Economics, founded in 1924.

The Institution maintains a position of neutrality on issues of public policy. Interpretations or conclusions in Brookings publications should be understood to be solely those of the authors.

Library of Congress Cataloging-in Publication data
Sequencing? Financial strategies for developing countries / Alison Harwood and
    Bruce L. R. Smith, editors.
    p. cm.
    Includes bibliographical reference and index.
    ISBN 0-8157-3498-0 (cloth : alk. paper). — ISBN 0-8157-3499-9 (pbk. : alk. paper)
    1. Finance—Developing countries.   2. Monetary policy—Developing countries.
    3. Financial institutions—Developing countries.
I. Harwood, Alison.   II. Smith, Bruce L. R.
HG195.R44   1997
332'.09172'4—dc21   96-48792
                                                              CIP

9 8 7 6 5 4 3 2 1

Typeset in Palatino

Composition by AlphaWebTech
Mechanicsville, Maryland

Printed by R. R. Donnelley and Sons, Co.
Harrisonburg, Virginia

Preface

The importance of the financial system in economic development was once frequently neglected by analysts and poorly understood by policymakers. A burgeoning scholarly literature, however, has recently begun to rectify the situation, focusing initially on the relationship between the financial system and monetary policy and exploring the links between financial crises and economic performance. But numerous gaps and uncertainties remain, and much more needs to be done. Further research is needed on a broad range of issues, including the role of the financial sector in economic growth, the appropriateness of different reform strategies, and the complexities of financial institution-building in an environment of economic liberalization.

The world's financial system has been buffeted in recent years by the crisis in the U.S. savings and loan industry, the implosion of the Japanese "bubble economy" of the late 1980s, the Mexican peso crisis, and other events. The trends toward globalization and economic liberalization have given rise to a host of complex new issues. There is no accepted wisdom that the industrial nations can readily confer on others, but the experiences of Western nations and of advanced developing nations in adapting to financial liberalization may provide useful insights for the many other countries embarking on a course of market reforms. Although liberalized financial systems are probably in general stronger and more robust than systems still operating under conditions of financial repression, important issues of equity, stability, efficiency, and safety present difficult challenges in the new environment to policymakers, regulators, the financial industry, and scholars.

The Brookings Institution, together with the KPMG Barents Group and supported by the U.S. Agency for International Development's Office of Emerging Markets, convened two conferences in October

v

and November 1994 to address this range of issues. Conference participants included representatives from the World Bank, from the International Monetary Fund, from private banks and consulting firms, both U.S. and foreign government officials, and finance experts from universities and the broader research community. The principal focus of the first conference was on financial services for poor people in the United States and abroad. The second conference dealt more generally and theoretically with financial reform and financial reform strategies in Asia, Latin America, eastern Europe, and Russia. This book presents the papers originally prepared for the second conference, all of which have been extensively revised by the authors in light of the conference discussions. The authors were charged to draw on their own extensive practical experience and to reflect the most recent research findings in their papers as well as to present their findings in a policy-relevant and readable form. They amply fulfilled our expectations and were a pleasure to work with. We thank them deeply for their efforts and for their patience.

We cannot acknowledge by name all of the others who provided valuable assistance, but we must mention several who were particularly helpful. From the Barents Group, J. D. Von Pischke helped launch the project and frame the issues, John Rogers was a source of encouragement and support, and Donna James provided administrative support. At Brookings, Michael Armacost, Lawrence Korb, and Robert Litan read and reviewed the manuscript, and Bruce MacLaury contributed advice on key points. Steph Selice skillfully edited the manuscript, Carlotta Ribar proofed the pages, Robert Elwood prepared the index, and Melton Castro designed the book jacket. The late LeeAnn Sonnergren of the Brookings Center for Public Policy Education and Susan Williams handled the logistics and organization of the conferences. Michael Voll served as research assistant and solved knotty computer problems, and Dennis Darnoi verified sources and references.

We gratefully acknowledge the financial support of the U.S. Agency for International Development, which made the project possible. In particular, we want to thank Rebecca Maestri of the AID Office of Emerging Markets for her wise counsel and collegiality throughout the effort.

The views expressed in this book, of course, are solely those of the individual authors and should not be ascribed to the U.S. Agency for International Development or to the trustees, officers, or other staff members of the Brookings Institution or the KPMG Barents Group.

Alison Harwood
Bruce L. R. Smith

Contents

Figures

Chapter 1

ALISON HARWOOD

Financial Reform in Developing Countries

Is there an optimal way to sequence the development of financial sectors? This question has attracted analytical interest and practical importance in recent years as observers have become more aware of the financial sector's significant role in economic development. With the increasing interest in market-oriented (as opposed to government-dominated) financial systems, it has become apparent that a vast amount of infrastructure is needed to support the financial sector and that it can take many years to build an adequate infrastructure. The limits on each country's time and resources, and the market risks and instability that can occur, reinforce the need to examine whether certain steps should be taken first to achieve orderly development and to effectively marshal a country's limited administrative resources. The introduction of the newly independent states of the former Soviet Union, and their need to transform rapidly their economies to market-oriented systems, has added impetus to the question of whether sequencing is viable and practical.

The debate about sequencing was started by Ronald McKinnon in the early 1970s. The focus then was on when in a country's economic development to start developing the financial system, rather than on the particular components of the financial system and their developmental sequence. As the importance of the financial system to economic development became clear, observers began to focus increasing attention on the system's various sectors. Early discussions tended to highlight the policies, laws, regulations, instruments, and institutions needed for an effective financial system—almost as if developing the infrastructure were as simple as adopting a new law or policy. Little recognition was initially given to how long it would take to build and integrate financial sector infrastructure so that it worked reasonably

1

well as a whole system. As a result, few insights were gained into the steps or the transition process by which a country would evolve to a well-functioning system.

In the past five years, experience has taught us how difficult and time consuming it is to build market infrastructure and what types of market instability and risks can result when new activities are introduced when the infrastructure is insufficient. This has raised questions of whether policymakers should encourage new activities if financial institutions, trading mechanisms, laws and regulations, and skilled market participants do not exist, or whether market activity can make do in the initial stages with limited infrastructure that can be built and refined with time.

These questions are addressed in this book. Drawing on the theoretical literature as well as on practical insights from development advisers, the authors of the chapters sought to determine whether there was an optimal path to financial development and reform of a financial sector. The initial chapters focus on issues concerning the speed of financial sector development, for sequencing is only an issue if some form of gradual development is followed. The authors also discuss the ability to control the process of change if a gradual approach is taken. Both points lead to the question of whether sequencing is ever feasible. A second set of chpaters covers the government's role in the financial system (that is, should the government just set prudent standards, or should it seek to influence economic outcomes). The authors discuss whether laws and regulations can or should follow in some sequence. The answers to the questions concerning the government's regulatory role strongly affect the timing and approach to increasing market power and introducing new financial services. Finally, several of the chapters explore questions concerning the introduction of new financial services and the infrastructure needed to support those services. Maxwell Fry's concluding chapter reviews the entire range of issues as they relate to the world's one hundred or so small economies.

The primary conclusion drawn in this book is that there is no optimal path to financial sector development. If we look at the historical record, it is clear that countries will waste time and opportunities trying to identify and pursue a universal or uniform correct path. Each country has underlying political, economic, sociological, legal, and institutional conditions that are unique to it, all of which will influence its development approach. Moreover, the development process is an unwieldy one, influenced by political considerations and broader issues of economic reform. The task should be approached opportunistically; steps should be taken when they can be in pragmatic terms. Adherence to theoretical precepts is neither practical nor desirable. In certain technical areas, there may be some limited opportunities to pursue a sequencing strategy—for instance, it may be best to have money markets before bond markets and to have government bond markets before corporate bond markets. Yet even in those cases, most of the authors in this book concur that moving forward should not be stalled because some theoretically identified prerequisite does not exist.

A fairly clear picture has emerged of what needs to be in place to have a well-functioning financial system, at least in terms of the types of services that should be offered and the range of supporting infrastructure needed. But though the overall goal and desired direction of change seem clear, there is less clarity on how to achieve the desired ends. Whatever approach a country follows will likely lead to problems and risks; the development process will never be smooth and without incident.

The important question to be asked is not what the optimal sequence is, but rather what set of practical conditions indicates an auspicious climate for any reform steps. A concomitant question is, what are the outcomes and risks that countries should be prepared to deal with as they move forward with the process of reform? More analytical work needs to be done to identify the conditions that indicate how a country might best proceed to develop its financial system and the risks to taking (and not taking) certain steps. Countries can then anticipate the problems they are likely to encounter and not overreact when they arise.

THE CONTEXT OF FINANCIAL SECTOR REFORM

The first question to address is the speed of change, for sequencing is only an issue if a gradual approach to development is followed. As is well known, there are two broad choices for the pace of change, and pros and cons with each choice. Broadly defined, the choices are broadly between gradualism and a "Big Bang," with the former typified by Asian countries such as Indonesia, Malaysia, Japan, and Korea and the latter by the transitional economies of the Eastern Bloc and newly independent states of the former Soviet Union. The trade-offs are most clearly examined in chapter 3 by R. Barry Johnston and the analytical commentary of Stephan Haggard in chapter 5.

The main benefits of gradualism are that it helps build consensus among parties involved in or influenced by the reform process. As Haggard argues, consensus and credibility help form a strong base for successful policy reforms, and sequencing reforms can gradually help build that base. Gradualism brings various parties into the debate and either co-opts them to a dominant view or incorporates and works through their concerns as the reform process proceeds. Not least of the virtues of gradualism is to get the parties to accept and abide by the changes that will be introduced. The "Big Bang," on the other hand, helps push through dislocations quickly and forces parties with vested interests to deal with and adjust to the new reality. As Haggard notes, swift action prevents rent-seekers from keeping the existing system working for them at the expense of others.

Both approaches have costs and risks that must be considered by each country to determine the most appropriate course of action. For example, Johnston argues that in the area of macroeconomics, the costs to following a gradualist policy can be low savings, capital flight, lack of monetary control, and inefficient resource allocation. But the risks to rapid liberalization can be market failure and instability resulting from the absence of adequate market infrastructure—laws and regulations to protect investor interests and guide participant behavior, well-informed regulators who can effectively supervise the market and enforce appropriate standards of behavior, sufficient mechanisms for handling market transactions, and financial institutions that understand how to perform their functions effectively and efficiently and handle client accounts honestly and accurately.

Johnston outlines several questions that countries should consider in trying to decide which option is best for them. One is whether the country can afford gradualism. The Japanese, he notes, could maintain a system of financial repression, because it did not reduce (and may have actually increased) their ability to mobilize savings for economic development. Some of the Southern Cone countries, in contrast, needed to liberalize rapidly to encourage greater mobilization of savings to finance development. Countries should also consider the impact financial sector reform may have on reform of other sectors of the economy. According to Johnston, the financial sector may be easier to reform than other sectors in some countries and can be a spur for liberalizing other sectors, such as the labor market.

Even if there were an optimal sequencing pattern or speed of reform, it is virtually inconceivable that a country could actually follow the pattern conscientiously in practice. Financial sector reform is not isolated; it is usually part of a broader stabilization or economic reform package, which must be pursued rapidly and across the board. Little time will be available to wait for preconditions to be put into place. Often financial reforms and "rereforms" will occur in response to broad-based problems or to initiatives of energetic policymakers. Balance of payments or banking crises can result in the introduction of new, more stringent policies and regulations in an effort to achieve economic stability or to deal with factors outside the financial system. Financial sector reform can thus be difficult to control and to pursue independently.

Fundamentally, financial sector reform everywhere is a political process influenced by personalities and power plays, not just economic theory and objectives. In the 1980s, the Japanese Ministry of Finance tried to stall financial liberalization to retain its control over particular policy areas and to prevent other ministries from gaining new powers. In other cases, strong vested interests have successfully lobbied politicians to retain protections. Governments may shy away from deregulating the banking system out of fear that weak but politically powerful banks will face failure and create a political crisis the governments do not want to deal with. Moreover, the development process often sits on a fragile foundation, with a strong likelihood of reversal that is difficult to prevent. Unlike in industrialized countries, where liberalization occurs because particular stakeholders push for it, in developing countries liberalization is often carried out under duress and in response to pressures from donors or from the international markets.

Finally, as Claudio Gonzalez-Vega notes in chapter 10 on nonbank financial institutions, financial sector development does not merely occur because of government actions. It is not just a top-down process but is often driven by market pressures for change. New institutions or activities are often introduced in response to customer demands ("upward pressure") or from financial institutions seeking to avoid regulation. The government is then forced to deal with this new reality, this new mix of financial services and institutions.

In sum, the development process is a complicated one—not always straightforward and logical, not purely economic, but riddled with various motives, personalities, and market pressures that influence the speed and direction of change. Consequently, trying to sequence or to rigidly control the process of financial sector development seems bound to fail. Furthermore, the process of reform is an opportunistic one; policymakers must exploit the windows of opportunity for change that crises create. If an opportunity arises that allows previously unpopular policy measures to be adopted, it would be foolish to delay because the step is not in accord with an ideal sequencing order—better to act and worry about policy adjustments later. As David C. Cole summarizes in chapter 4: "Theoretical propositions about, or empirical searches for, optimal sequences for macroeconomic policy reforms are not only likely to be unrewarding, they can actually be counterproductive if they suggest to politicians and policymakers that it is inappropriate to carry out an important macroeconomic policy reform if some other macroeconomic policy change has not yet been implemented."

THE GOVERNMENT'S ROLE

The role played by government in the financial system is a critical dimension. The order and speed with which government controls ("economic regulation") are decreased, markets liberalized, and prudential regulations introduced remain vital issues, even though most countries are striving to build market-oriented rather than government-controlled financial systems. There is a need for economic and prudential regulation in the transition from a regulated to a deregulated environment. Hence I will discuss the interaction between prudential regulations and liberalization measures and then focus on the legal framework for the financial sector.

Observers in the early years of promoting market-oriented financial systems extolled the virtues of the market while denigrating almost all forms of government intervention. The underlying assumption was that governments were imperfect (which they had amply demonstrated throughout the 1960s and 1970s) and that markets were perfect. The implication was that markets should be free from government control and left to their own devices to determine who should participate in them and what the economic outcome of such participation would be. In hindsight, this view of markets ignored both the history of market instability in developed countries and the fact that young markets generally tend to be unstable because of their lack of infrastructure.

The 1980s highlighted the serious problems that developed markets can face and thus provided useful experience for emerging market countries. As Lawrence J. White argues in chapter 6, today there is greater understanding that real-world policy choices are between imperfect markets and imperfect governments. As markets are liberalized and as economic regulation is reduced, the government must set and enforce prudential standards of behavior for market participants (see Betty F. Slade in chapter 8 on the need for these prudential regulations). This raises two related sequencing issues: when to transition away from economic regulation, and how to sequence the introduction of prudential regulations and liberalization.

Even if countries know they want to build a market-oriented financial system where the government's main role is as a prudential regulator, the question remains of how to get to that point. Countries that choose to evolve gradually, removing direct controls piece by piece, usually do so because they fear that the markets are immature (that is, more imperfect than the government) and incapable of producing "good" economic decisions. There are different ways of addressing this fear and of moving toward the point where the market can take on an increasingly larger role in pricing and allocating capital. The approach that diverges most from the philosophy of a market-oriented system is to have "economic regulation" where the government influences outcomes such as access to and price of funds for the borrowers. The Japanese government, for example, allowed securities markets to develop; however, for many years it employed "merit" regulation to limit and control who could borrow in the markets, how much, and at what price. The Ministry of Finance set financial ratios that Japanese corporations had to meet to issue bonds and set the interest rates that various ratios would merit. A company whose ratios put it in the highest category might be able to borrow 5-year paper at a 10 percent interest rate, whereas a company in the second-highest category might have to pay 12 percent. This approach helped limit market risk, direct funds, and control interest rates—all areas the Japanese government did not trust to the market.

The second, more common approach is to impose varying degrees of prudential regulations on financial institutions such as banks and securities firms, to limit the risk that their actions pose to the market and to investors. This includes requiring capital to absorb losses, mandating that professionals be licensed, and the like. The degree of these measures will vary with time and stage of development. In chapter 4 Cole outlines some of the steps countries might take in moving from more restrictive to intermediate and then to liberalized policy regimes (for monetary policy, exchange rates, prudential supervision, and the like). In the early stages of financial sector development, for instance, a country's monetary policy may be controlled by expanding and contracting central bank credit. In the intermediate stage, as the economy and financial system become more liberalized and commercial banking activities grow, reserve requirements and direct control of reserve money is used to carry out monetary policy. In the more liberalized systems, the more indirect, open market operations become the primary tool for monetary management. At each successive stage, as the government gains more confidence in market-based operations, it supplants direct mechanisms with indirect ones.

How fast countries evolve from restrictive to intermediate to liberalized systems will depend on how willing the government is to let go of direct controls. This in turn depends on such factors as how risk averse the government is, and how capable the market is of meeting the economy's needs. This latter factor partly depends on how well developed the government's infrastructure is, and how capable the government is in bringing about "good" economic outcomes—which in turn partly depends on how capable the bureaucracy is and how much it can operate outside the political system. The relative strengths and weaknesses of the government and the market will therefore play a large role in how quickly direct controls can be replaced with indirect ones. Instead of an optimal approach to removing regulations, there is a need to understand the nuances and particulars of the local situation.

In chapter 8 Slade discusses the importance of prudential regulation as a recognized feature of any well-functioning market, and when those regulations should best be introduced relative to measures to liberalize market activities. Is there an optimal sequence for introducing prudential regulations and liberalization measures, to avoid the ever-so-commonly seen cycle of liberalization followed by crisis and then prudential regulation? Logic suggests that prudential regulations should be in place and operational before markets are liberalized, to guide the behavior of market participants in the more liberalized environment and limit their risk taking.

But this approach is not always followed. In chapter 9 Gerard Caprio, Jr., argues that the banking sector has actually seen perverse regulation. Policymakers often focus on adopting the more visible aspects of reform, such as deregulating interest rates or creating stock exchanges, before regulations governing the behavior of institutions operating in these new activities are in place and operational. This "perversion," in which liberalization occurs before effective regulation and supervision is in place, helps explain the plethora of banking crises that have plagued countries throughout the emerging-market world.

Yet the same conditions can lead to different reactions. First, there is a question of whether a country can or actually will work according to the perceived logic. Cole argues that countries often need to use "reverse" regulation. Policymakers are often stretched so thin they will not deal with developing prudential regulations until there is an absolute need to do so—that is, until a crisis. Even if the regulations are introduced alongside liberalization measures, effective enforcement takes a long time to develop (as Caprio argues in chapter 9, as does Philip A. Wellons in somewhat similar fashion in chapter 7). To have effective enforcement in place when liberalization measures are introduced means starting to build enforcement capabilities months or even years before the activities to be regulated are introduced. Even countries that have the time to address these issues before they become crises might find it difficult to do that successfully. What makes most sense logically may therefore not always work in practice.

Furthermore, countries run the risk of choking private sector activity if they introduce prudential regulations too quickly, particularly if the regulations are stringent and complicated. Prudential regulations should instead be introduced dynamically and interactively with market developments. They should be stringent enough at any point to guide behavior and assure some quality of transactions, but also simple enough to be understood and leave enough breathing room for economic activities to thrive.

The importance of a legal framework to the well-functioning, market-oriented financial system in a broad sense is recognized and accepted today. The legal framework sets standards of behavior for market participants, details the rights and responsibilities of transacting parties, assures that completed transactions are legally binding, and gives regulators the teeth to enforce standards and ensure compliance with and adherence to the law. Without an adequate legal framework, a country cannot expect to develop confidence and interest in its financial transactions, or for the financial entities to have confidence in themselves. Individual parties can bring the entire financial system to its knees because of greed or poor management.

Yet the scope of laws and regulations needed to support a so-called well-functioning financial system is even more extensive than is commonly understood. The laws alone include those for economic transactions, such as commercial codes, contract law, and trust law, as well as those specific to financial transactions, such as securities, banking, and insurance laws, to name but a few. These are in addition to the prudential regulations specific to each area of economic activity, as well as the regulations governing the operations of particular institutions such as stock exchanges and clearing corporations. Not surprisingly, developing this body of laws and regulations takes years, leaving the financial system with important holes in the certainty and transparency of key activities.

Given the importance of and time frames involved in developing the legal and regulatory framework, the question is whether its development and introduction can be sequenced so that the most important elements are addressed first and a semblance of order maintained in the financial system as new activities are introduced. In his discussion of this topic, Wellons notes that there are two sequencing areas to consider: legal content and legal process. A natural sequence may be in the legal process: laws are first enacted, then implemented, then enforced. But developing any sequence in legal content is difficult, and Wellons analyzes the reasons why—many having to do with lack of coordination across competing ministries and advisers and the normal vicissitudes of the political process. Ministries typically operate in a vacuum, without a vision of how their actions fit within the broader picture and without time or incentive to think about what is being done elsewhere. In many cases, the process is too unwieldy and too politicized to control effectively. Champions will emerge in one policy area or another and push the fortunes of their ministers. Wellons argues, however, that some general prescriptions can be made about sequencing the development of legal content. The starting point is to determine whether to first write laws specifically related to the financial system (securities or banking laws) or laws that affect the financial system (commercial codes, trust laws, or contract law). The next logical issue is to specify the type of financial system that the legal framework is to support—that is, a credit-based, indirect system or a market-based, direct system. Each will have its own package of laws and regulations needed to support it. However, Wellons concedes that, beyond at least private property, he does not see any inherent sequence to developing numerous subcomponents of a legal regime (bankruptcy, securities law, and the like). They are all important and should be developed as soon as possible, the order to be dictated by practicality and political feasibility.

If a country decides to develop a mix of economic and financial system laws, it has two broad choices: develop each category of law in its entirety (that is, write the commercial code first, then the banking law, then the trust law, and so on) or, alternatively, select a "core" set of elements for each category needed in the early stages of activity and proceed with this bundle of core elements. Both approaches have their benefits and risks, with the second approach probably winning out. The benefit of the second approach is the simplicity of the legal content, which means quicker understanding by all parties involved as well as faster implementation and enforcement. The risk, according to Wellons, is that abuses and confusion begin early and can escalate beyond remedy. A country may end up with a law or regulation on its books that invites perverse behavior.

One way to provide flexibility to change rules is to develop regulations rather than laws first and put the necessary details in the regulations, as regulations can be changed quickly to address new circumstances. But the confusion spawned by excessive decrees claiming to have the force of law, and the lack of clarity about hierarchy of law in post-communist nations, is a caution against decrees. Moreover, it is clear that the financial reform should not drive legal development. Establishing the rule of law in transitional societies is clearly more important than enacting financial regulations that cannot be enforced or administered in an uncertain legal case.

In the final outcome, each country will have to pick its own mix of simple but broad-based or narrow but complete laws and rules based on its own circumstances. Although there is no optimal approach, there are questions that all countries should address: whether they want to support a direct or indirect financial system; whether the government has the political commitment and ability to move to a market economy; and whether government or the market should allocate credit.

DEVELOPING AND REFORMING FINANCIAL SYSTEMS

The discussion of building legal infrastructure highlights issues that are equally relevant to developing and reforming new and existing financial systems—banking, capital markets, pensions and insurance, and nonbank financial institutions. The need to develop infrastructure to support these activities is a critical concern in when and how fast to introduce them. Here too we find that there is no optimal approach to development. Instead, why a country wants something developed and what the situation in that country is will influence when and how the development should proceed.

The question of when to introduce new financial services relative to one other seems difficult to answer. In chapter 2 Ross Levine sees a typical pattern in many developing countries, where banks develop first, then capital markets, and finally specialized financial institutions such as pension funds and insurance companies. Clearly, banking is the most basic financial service and forms the beginning of a financial system nearly everywhere. Markets, such as securities markets, emerge as economic growth raises the need to attract and allocate more funds. New, alternative instruments arise to attract funds and serve the needs of new borrowers and lenders. As the economy grows, so does the wealth of individuals and of corporations, which can begin focusing not just on meeting today's needs but on saving for tomorrow's (as is discussed in Dimitri Vittas's chapter 11 on pensions and insurance).

The question of when to introduce new nonbank financial services also is influenced by why those services are desired. The "why" may be broader and more complex than we have previously thought. That is, when we think about the question of why to reform areas such as banking and capital markets, the objective has usually been to mobilize and allocate more capital. But countries that are growing need a deeper, more diversified financial system to support the growth, and a more diversified economy. Mobilizing capital is only one function to be served by the financial system.

Financial services perform other central financial functions, such as risk management, and help shape important institutional practices such as corporate governance practices. When and how the services will take shape in given countries or regions is uncertain. For example, the impetus for capital market development in Asia has typically been to provide alternative sources of funding and investment for a growing and increasingly diversified economy. But in Central and Eastern Europe and the states of the former Soviet Union, the need to support privatization movements has been decisive. The Russian economy may not have needed equity markets for funding purposes a few years ago, but it needed the capital market institutions to support privatization measures. The "why" has therefore influenced the "how." When capital markets are introduced to provide alternative funding sources, the typical sequence seen is introduction of policies to encourage the flow of funds to equity issuers, building trading mechanisms to encourage trades and create market liquidity (to encourage more investment and more issuance), then developing clearing and settlement systems and registrars. When the impetus is privatization, we may instead first see registrars developed to assure that the public's ownership of companies is registered, then clearing mechanisms to support informal trades of those shares, and finally trading systems to encourage greater trading and a more liquid market that will ultimately provide a funding source for the newly privatized enterprises.

In addition to providing funding sources or supporting privatization, capital markets also serve another important function: to improve corporate governance and help institutionalize transparency and public disclosure. Companies that were tightly held and secretive are pushed to provide information to the public or else lose access to the capital market. As more companies decide to use the market, the concept of Western-style public disclosure takes hold. The public begins to realize that it has rights as shareholders of the companies and demands a form of economic democracy from them. Corporate governance and public disclosure are thus by-products of capital market development; this role in some countries may be more important than the funding role. All this is to say that the decision on when to start developing capital markets should not just be based on when a country needs a nonbank-funding vehicle.

Introduction of new financial services can also arise in response to customer demands or from market participants trying to avoid regulation, rather than from conscious policy choices. In those circumstances, as Gonzalez-Vega observes in chapter 10, there is no optimal sequencing—sequence, in fact, becomes irrelevant. No one is controlling the process. Once new services are introduced from these upward pressures or regulatory avoidance, the government has to deal with an entirely new mix or context when thinking about introducing other new activities.

Finally, the emergence of new financial services is also considerably influenced by whether the infrastructure exists to support the activity. The infrastructure needed to support financial services is clearly extensive and takes time to develop. In addition to the body of laws and regulations addressed in the last section, it includes financial intermediaries such as banks, securities firms, and insurance companies; market transaction mechanisms and institutions such as stock exchanges, trading systems, clearinghouses, and registrars; and information sources such as credit rating agencies and accounting systems that provide standardized, useful information on borrowers.

Not only do these institutions and mechanisms need to exist, they need to have some degree of capability. Institution staffs need to be skilled, accounting standards need to be understood and followed, and trading systems need to function. Clearly, the level of that functioning can be built and developed with time. But governments and market participants have to balance the desire for new services with the reality of whether enough infrastructure exists to ensure some degree of quality in those services. Answering this question poses the same concerns as those discussed earlier regarding how fast to proceed (see Johnston in chapter 3).

It is clear that infrastructure is critical but time consuming. One sensible approach is to keep it simple. As with the laws and regulations, what needs to be done is to understand the approaches that can be used to developing infrastructure, the risks of waiting and of not waiting, and the different growth patterns (when is it best to start with a manual trading system and replace it with an automated one or to wait until an automated one is in place; how to involve skilled insurance agents; and so on). Governments and market participants have to balance the desire for new services with the reality of whether enough infrastructure exists to provide some degree of quality in those services. In any case, an approach that is best for one country will not necessarily be best for another.

CONCLUSIONS

In the final analysis, there is no ideal way to develop a financial system for all countries. As most of the authors in this book conclude, the quest is misplaced both as an analytical goal and as a realistic policy concern. A country's particular conditions and circumstances—its macroeconomics; financial, legal, and political systems; sociology; and strength of its government relative to the market—will influence the steps it should take and govern the order and speed of the policy steps in any reform of the financial system. Consequently, there are many different sequencing options to choose from. The challenge for governments, as Cole asserts in chapter 4, is "to implement a mix of [policy] regimes that suits the country's circumstances at the given time, and to move the regimes over time to fit the long-run needs of the country," rather than to look for one rigid approach. Even if we knew what the basic guides are to development—and what countries ideally need in order to have a well-functioning financial system—we are still unclear on the transition from current reality to the desired end.

The process of financial sector development will never be a smooth one. It is by nature unwieldy and difficult to control, driven by market vagaries and affected by a country's political and social institutions. Both taking action or taking none at all will pose risks, and the ability to shape evolving priorities may be limited.

Countries will need to know what those risks are and how to anticipate and prepare for them, so they do not overregulate and choke the development process. More research and chronicling should be done to identify which conditions help determine when a country might want to take a particular action, what the options to action and the risks of those various options are and how they might best be handled, and what the outcomes are likely to be. The goal would be to identify which other countries have the most relevant experience for a given country at the particular time, and to use the experience of those countries as a guide to behavior, rather than a purely functional, technical approach to selecting actions.

A second line of research is needed to identify the core elements to infrastructure (legal, regulatory, institutional, human-capital skills, and so on) that might be in put in place at different stages of development, and how to build on them with time. Of course, these actions would also be subject to the same comments about sequencing made here, and the conditions and risks of moving would need to be clearly identified.

All emerging market countries like to think they are unique, dealing with their differing circumstances and concerns. In many respects they are. But the experiences of other countries can provide useful insights and guidance on how to manage the process of reform to make it as effective and risk free as possible.

Chapter 2

ROSS LEVINE

Financial Functions, Institutions, and Growth

In this chapter I first broadly discuss the relationship between financial sector development and economic growth and argue that a well-functioning financial system promotes long-run economic growth, so that implementing sound financial sector policies should be a high priority on policymakers' agendas. Next I present preliminary research results on comparative patterns of financial system development. In particular, I draw on my work with Asli Demirguc-Kunt that illustrates a similar cross-country pattern of financial development. We have found that as countries get richer, the credit-allocating function of central banks becomes less important, and private banks become more so. The fraction of credit allocated to private firms rises; later, stock markets blossom and nonbank financial intermediaries like insurance companies, mutual funds, and pension funds flourish.[1] This pattern, in turn, seems to imply a financial policy sequencing strategy: to follow the "natural" path of development, poorer countries should focus on implementing sound policies, regulations, and supervisory systems that encourage banks to develop, while middle-income countries should also construct an adequate policy, legal, and regulatory environment for capital market and nonbank development.

But this apparently logical sequence may be misleading. The link between the broad empirical trends observed in our study and the sequence of financial reforms that a country should pursue are not quite as simple as this pattern suggests. In the third part of this chapter I discuss the economics profession's understanding of the links in the chain from financial sector policies, to the structure and functioning of the financial system, and then to overall economic growth. Inadequate understanding makes it difficult for the profession to provide rigorously grounded advice on an array of financial policy issues, especially regulatory ones.

FINANCE AND GROWTH

The importance of the financial system is often underappreciated. Although much influential work emphasizes the role of the financial system in economic development, financial development is frequently not a mainstay of development research nor the focus of development policy advice.[2] For example, in a recent survey of development economics, Nicholas Stern does not mention financial development.[3] Impressively, at the end of Stern's review, he lists numerous topics he lacked sufficient space to cover; finance is not even listed among those omitted. Also, a reader who browses through a development economics textbook will typically find only oblique references to financial sector issues. Many of these allusions involve the ties between the financial system and monetary policy, or the links between financial crises and economic performance. There is little discussion of the ties between the financial system and economic growth over decades.

This underemphasis ignores important recent theoretical and empirical work that stresses the relevance of the financial sector in economic growth. Consider the question of whether the level of financial development predicts future long-run economic growth. To address this, Robert King and I studied the growth experiences of about eighty countries over the period 1960–89.[4] We constructed many different measures of financial development. Because these financial development measures tell the same story, I simply present the results using the most widely used measure of financial development—DEPTH, which measures the overall size of the formal financial sector.[5] Specifically, DEPTH equals currency held outside financial institutions plus demand deposits and interest-bearing liabilities of banks and nonbank financial intermediaries, divided by gross domestic product (GDP).[6] The presumption underlying the use of this measure of financial development is that the size of the formal financial sector is positively associated with the provision of financial services. I define and discuss these services below.

In our study we rank countries by the value of DEPTH in 1960, starting with countries with the smallest level of financial development and then those with the greatest financial development in 1960.[7] We then break the countries into four groups of twenty countries each. Countries with very small DEPTH measures fall into the first group; countries with huge financial development in 1960 fall into the fourth group. For each of these four groups of countries, figure 2-1 presents the rate of real per capita GDP growth over the next thirty years.

As illustrated, countries with larger financial systems in 1960 grew more quickly over the section of countries. Much more rigorous statistical analysis confirms the pattern in figure 2-1: level of financial development is a good predictor of overall economic growth over subsequent decades. I therefore read the evidence as strongly suggesting that, if we can derive good financial sector policies, we can stimulate sustained economic growth.

COMPARATIVE PATTERNS OF FINANCIAL AND ECONOMIC DEVELOPMENT

Does the structure of the financial system differ systematically across countries with varying levels of income per capita? This question gave rise to Raymond Goldsmith's pathbreaking book *Financial Structure and Development*.[8] Demirguc-Kunt and I follow Goldsmith in defining financial structure as the combination of a country's financial institutions and financial markets.[9] Financial structures differ in the sense that various institutions and markets are differentially important across countries. The overall size of the financial system may also differ across countries.

Based on the approach Demirguc-Kunt and I took, five variables illustrate how the size and structure of financial systems differ across countries. The overall size of the financial system is first measured using DEPTH (which is defined as currency held outside financial institutions plus demand deposits and interest-bearing liabilities of banks and nonbank financial intermediaries divided by GDP). Second, the importance of banks—as opposed to the central bank—in allocating credit is assessed (using the concept of BANK SHARE, bank credit divided by bank credit plus central bank credit). The role of the

FIGURE 2-1. *Financial Depth in 1960 and Growth from 1960 to 1989*

Annual per capita GDP growth, 1960–89

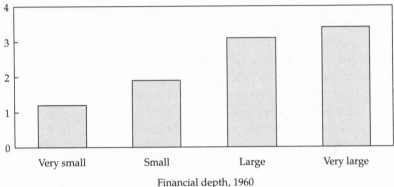

Financial depth, 1960

financial system in allocating credit to private firms—as opposed to funding government deficits or public enterprises—is then measured using the variable PRIVATE SHARE (credit issued to private sector firms divided by total credit). Fourth, the role of nonbanks (insurance companies, pension funds, mutual funds, brokerage houses, and investment banks) is measured using the variable NONBANK SHARE (nonbank assets divided by GDP). Finally, the level of stock market development is measured by using a combination of variables designed to measure the size of the stock market relative to total economic activity, the liquidity of the market, and the degree of integration with world capital markets.

Figure 2-2 depicts a distinct pattern as we move from poorer to richer countries. The highlights of this figure include the following trends:

—Financial systems get larger;

—Banks grow in importance relative to the central bank in allocating credit;

—The financial system allocates a larger share of total credit to private firms;

—Nonbanks grow in importance; and

—Stock markets become more developed.

These results are subject to numerous data problems. For example, it is difficult to distinguish private from public banks and development

FIGURE 2-2. *Financial Structure for Countries at Different Income Per Capita Levels*

Financial indicators

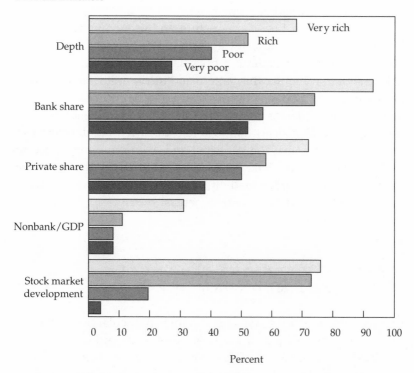

Percent

banks from commercial banks in many settings. Similarly, the definitions of a bank and of a nonbank are not always consistent across
countries. It is also worth noting that many differences exist across
countries at similar stages of economic development. For example, the
assets of deposit banks accounted for 56 percent of financial system
assets in France, while the comparable number in the United Kingdom
was 35 percent. The assets of contractual savings institutions composed 26 percent of total financial system assets in the United Kingdom, while in France the figure was only 7 percent in 1985. Though
there is a general trend involving financial structure and the level of
GDP per capita, there are thus exceptions and differences within the
categories presented in figure 2-2. One additional caveat must be
noted: The lines of causation in these findings are unclear. Figure 2-2

is merely an indication of an association between financial structure and economic development. The figure does not imply that somehow changing the structure of the financial system in a particular pattern will result in countries becoming richer.

The link between financial structure and economic development depicted in figure 2-2 may, however, have policy interpretations. For example, if there is a pattern to financial development, then policy-makers should recognize this pattern and incorporate it into financial reform programs. Poorer countries might thus be encouraged to focus on developing their banking systems first, while middle-income countries might adopt policies that facilitate stock market development. These conclusions may be plausible and even tempting, but I am cautious, particularly given my assessment of where the profession stands in terms of understanding the links between financial sector policies and the functioning of the financial system.

LINKS BETWEEN THE FINANCIAL SYSTEM AND ECONOMIC GROWTH

Are there policy reforms, sequenced in some particular order, that will promote the functioning of the financial system and thereby boost sustained economic growth? The question must be framed so as to focus on financial functions, services provided by the financial system, the real value the system adds, and what the system does. The focus of policy analyses should not be on particular financial institutions, markets, or instruments per se. Financial intermediaries and markets should be viewed as vehicles for providing financial services.

The challenge for economists is to explore how financial sector policies, regulations, and supervision affect financial institutions, markets, and instruments, and how these changes affect financial services and long-run economic growth. Resolving this challenge is critical for good country-specific policy advice. Because it is entirely likely in theory and clearly evident in practice that different financial structures—combinations of financial institutions and markets—can provide similar qualities and quantities of financial services, we must have an organized way of defining, measuring, and analyzing how financial sector policies influence (or fail to influence) the structure and functioning of the financial system.

In evaluating the economics profession's understanding of the links from financial policies to financial services and ultimately to economic growth, the focus of effort has traditionally been on the last link. Economists have defined the central functions performed by the financial system and dissected the conceptual linkages between these functions and economic activity. The five financial functions commonly discussed are (1) risk management, including managing liquidity risk; (2) researching and evaluating firms, projects, and managers; (3) corporate governance, or monitoring of managers and firms to whom money has been lent; (4) mobilizing savings in society; and (5) facilitating transactions. These financial functions may affect long-run economic growth through two channels: by influencing the savings rate and by affecting capital allocation.

First, economists have focused on two types of risk: liquidity risk and idiosyncratic or diversification-type risk. Liquidity risk is the risk associated with selling an asset: is there a market, is it easy to sell, and are executable prices readily available? Real estate, for example, is generally less liquid and experiences more liquidity risk than government Treasury bills. Idiosyncratic risk is the risk associated with a particular firm going bust, or an industry enduring losses, or the investments in a particular country all doing poorly. Some people generally do not like risk. Financial systems price risk and provide mechanisms for pooling, ameliorating, and trading it. Recent uses of options and futures contracts to hedge and trade interest rate and exchange rate risk have been well publicized.

At a more basic level, financial institutions transform asset and liability maturities to satisfy savers and investors. The securities most useful to businesses—equities, bonds, bills of exchange—may not have the liquidity, security, and risk avoidance characteristics that savers desire. By offering attractive financial instruments to savers— liquid demand deposits and mutual funds diversified across firms, industries, and countries—financial intermediaries can tailor financial instruments for different clients and thereby manage risk for individuals. By facilitating the management, trading, and pooling of risk, financial systems can ease the interactions between savers and investors.

Financial systems that provide risk management services and financial markets that reduce liquidity risk will encourage efficient resource allocation. For example, Bencivenga and Smith, Levine, and Obstfeld have shown that on average financial instruments, markets, and institutions that minimize risk will tend to cause savings to flow toward these higher-return, innovation-producing investments.[10] The effects on the savings rate are commonly ambiguous in these models because of the unknown effects of uncertainty on savings. An historical example involving liquidity risk illustrates the importance of risk management. One of the first joint stock companies in England was formed in 1609. What was remarkable about this company was that the owners originally gave their capital to the company but could not ask for it back later! For this to be attractive to potential equity holders, there had to a reasonably liquid secondary market to sell shares. The development of secondary equity markets in England thus helped promote the growth of companies with secure, permanent capital bases.

In addition, economists have analyzed the individual financial system's capacity to obtain information, evaluate firms, and allocate capital. Because firms, projects, and managers are difficult to evaluate, savers may not have the time, resources, or means to collect and process information on a wide array of enterprises, markets, managers, and economic conditions. Financial intermediaries can therefore obtain and evaluate information and allocate capital based on these assessments. Many firms and entrepreneurs will solicit capital; financial intermediaries that are better at selecting the most promising firms and managers will spur economic growth by fostering a more efficient allocation of capital.

We have formally modeled this intuition.[11] This view, however, goes back at least to Walter Bagehot, editor of the *Economist*, who observed of Lombard Street, London's financial center, almost one hundred twenty-five years ago: "[England's financial] organization is so useful because it is so easily adjusted. Political economists say that capital sets towards the most profitable trades, and that it rapidly leaves the less profitable and non-paying trades. But in ordinary countries this is a slow process. . . . In England, however, . . . capital runs as surely and instantly where it is most wanted, and where there is most to be made of it, as water runs to find its level."[12] Bagehot was describing in the mid-1800s one of the factors behind England's comparative economic success: the ability of England's financial system to identify and fund the most profitable industries more quickly than other countries' financial systems could.

Financial intermediaries also provide an important dimension of corporate governance through the time-consuming and costly function of evaluating the performance of firm managers. Consequently, financial intermediaries often compel managers to act in the best interests of stock-, debt-, and loanholders. In brief, financial intermediaries help resolve the principal-agent problem by enhancing the limited capacity of claimholders to oversee the actions of their managers.

Without this role in corporate governance, managers would allocate firm resources in accord with their own interests, not the interests of shareholders and debtholders. Recourse allocation would be less efficient and economies would grow more slowly. In addition, in the absence of sound corporate governance, savers would be less willing to invest in large corporations. This reluctance could lower overall savings or encourage smaller, more easily monitored firms, which would mean less economic efficiency. Effective financial systems will prompt managers to allocate resources more efficiently, thereby promoting long-run growth.

In addition to risk amelioration, resource allocation, and corporate governance, financial systems also serve to mobilize resources within society for productive ends. Some worthwhile investment projects may require large capital inputs, and many projects enjoy economics of scale. By agglomerating savings, financial intermediaries aid markets and enlarge the set of feasible investment projects and thus encourage economic efficiency. Greenwood and Smith have formally modeled this intuition.[13] However, once again they observe that this critical role for the financial system was noted much earlier by Bagehot: "We have entirely lost the idea that any undertaking likely to pay, and seen to be likely, can perish for want of money; yet no idea was more familiar to our ancestors, or is more common in most countries. A citizen of Long in Queen Elizabeth's time . . . would have thought that it was no use inventing railways (if he could have understood what a railway meant), for you would have not been able to collect the capital with which to make them. At this moment, in colonies and all rude countries, there is no large sum of transferable money; there is not fund from which you can borrow, and out of which you can make immense works."[14]

By effectively mobilizing resources for sound investment projects, the financial system may play a crucial role in permitting the adoption of better technologies, thus promoting economic development. However, this function of resource mobilization is only one of many, and its significance should not be exaggerated. For example, analysts have argued that stock markets are less important than banks, because not much corporate capital is raised through stock markets, even in countries where they are well developed. One weakness of this argument is that stock markets may provide other functions (such as risk management opportunities) that promote growth.[15] The point is that resource mobilization is one of several important functions performed by the financial systems.

Finally, financial systems facilitate trade. At the most rudimentary level, money minimizes the need for barter and encourages commerce and specialization, as Adam Smith argued more than two hundred years ago. At a more sophisticated level, checks, credit cards, and the entire payments and clearance mechanisms simplify a wide array of economic interactions. In most industrialized economies, individuals and businesses take the ability to write and settle financial transactions for granted. But the absence of a reliable means for conducting trade significantly impedes economic activity and slows economic growth. This is exemplified most notably in transitional socialist economies, where insufficiently developed payments and clearance systems have stymied economic interactions. In sum, financial systems make trade and commerce easy, foster economic activity, and promote economic growth by encouraging and supporting the more efficient allocation of resources.

POLICY, LEGAL, AND REGULATORY FRAMEWORK

Although economists have been relatively successful at rigorously dissecting the links between the services provided by the financial system and economic growth, the profession has had varying degrees of success in fully articulating the ties between an array of financial sector policies and regulations and long-run growth. In term of relative successes, the economics profession has extensively studied the effects of lowering direct and indirect taxes on financial intermediaries and of relaxing interest rate and credit controls. There are formal economic models that show how taxing intermediaries, controlling interest rates, and misdirecting credit can reduce savings rates, hinder the efficient allocation of savings, and slow economic growth. Furthermore, Roubini and Sala-I-Martin, and Bencivenga and Smith, have developed sophisticated models of why economies with poor tax systems often optimally resort to financial repression.[16] Financial repression is thus not a mistake in these models; financial repression is the optimal policy choice given the options available for raising revenue.

In contrast, economists have no correspondingly extensive set of theories on how regulations governing capital requirements, restrictions on the range of activities performed by particular intermediaries, insurance of financial intermediary liabilities, investor protection laws, or information disclosure requirements affect long-run economic growth.

In terms of empirical work on financial liberalization, there are both weaknesses and some notable strengths cited in the literature. With regard to weaknesses, our inability to achieve precise definitions and qualitative measurements of financial functions makes it difficult to assess how financial liberalization affects the functioning of the financial system. However, there have been advances in illustrating some of the benefits and pitfalls of financial liberalization. In a book edited by Caprio, firm-level evidence from Ecuador and Indonesia shows that following financial liberalization, banks redirected the flow of credit from firms that were less efficient to those that are more efficient.[17] Although there was little change in the savings rate in Ecuador and Indonesia, there was a more efficient allocation of savings following liberalization.

In books by Caprio, Vittas, and Brock, case studies more generally suggest one further significant finding regarding the connection between liberalization and financial reform.[18] Financial liberalization, it appears, will succeed (that is, will promote the provision of high-quality financial services) only when it is accompanied by a sound regulatory and supervisory system. Although not always defined explicitly, regulatory and supervisory systems are frequently referred to as "sound" when official supervisors and regulators have the incentives and capabilities to monitor rigorously the investment and financing activities of financial intermediaries, and when supervisory and regulatory policies also create incentives—and reduce disincentives—for private sector participants to also monitor financial intermediaries. These authors argue that financial liberalization in the absence of a sound regulatory and supervisory system has typically set the stage for future financial crises. The upgrading of regulatory and supervisory systems is therefore suggested as a prerequisite for financial liberalization. A major weakness of this conclusion is that we do not have sufficiently detailed empirical measures of what constitutes a sound regulatory and supervisory system.

CONCLUSIONS

Clearly, a country's general legal framework will influence the structure and functioning of financial intermediaries and markets. For example, it would be difficult to have an options market if these contracts were not defined as binding legal obligations within the context of a national legal system. Similarly, Mexico's legal and regulatory system defines a holding company structure such that banks, insurance companies, brokerage firms, and the like may be included as subsidiaries under the financial holding company. A different legal and regulatory system would create another financial structure. This much is clear. However, when addressing the next part of the chain—the effect of different financial structures on the provision and quality of financial functions—the analytical terrain becomes murky. Are universal banks better at providing financial services, or is a holding company structure superior?

Similarly, we are still searching for satisfying answers to questions associated with the effects of different regulatory policies on the provision of financial services. What effects do different types of deposit insurance—or other types of implicit and explicit government guarantees on pension funds, insurance companies, mutual funds, and so on—have on the provision of financial services? What is the effect on financial services when a government tries to boost its domestic stock market, versus allowing domestic firms to list in New York, or London, or Tokyo? The effects of various types of financial reform on the financial structure and how the resultant change in the financial structure affects the provision of key financial functions are difficult to assess. The research community is still struggling to clarify these issues and to define its research agenda.

Because financial sector development appears to be an important predictor of future economic growth, financial sector policy issues should be of great interest to policy analysts and policymakers. A pattern of joint financial and economic development is also discernible across a broad range of countries, whereby central banks shrink in importance and banks rise in importance as countries get richer; subsequently, nonbanks and stock markets blossom. However, this joint financial and economic development pattern does not suggest that countries can accelerate economic growth by changing the structure of their financial systems.

In addition, researchers are starting to piece together answers regarding the links from financial sector policies to the structure of the financial system, to services provided by the financial system, and finally to economic growth. The weakest link in the chain is that between the structure of the financial system and the services provided by it. Gaining a better understanding of the effects of various types of financial regulation on the financial structure and how the resultant change in this structure affects key financial functions is critical to improving our policy advice and promoting sustained economic development.

REFERENCES

Bagehot, Walter. 1873 (1962 edition). *Lombard Street*. Homewood, Ill.: Richard D. Irwin.
Bencivenga, Valerie R., and Bruce D. Smith. 1991. "Financial Intermediation and Endogenous Growth." *Review of Economic Studies* 58 (April): 195–209.
―――. 1992. "Deficits, Inflation and the Banking System in Developing Countries: The Optimal Degree of Financial Repression." *Oxford Economic Papers* 44 (October): 767–90.
Brock, Philip L., ed. 1992. *If Texas Were Chile: A Primer on Banking Reform*. San Francisco: CA-ICS Press.
Cameron, Rondo, and others. 1967. *Banking in the Early Stages of Industrialization: A Study in Comparative Economic History*. Oxford University Press.

Caprio, Jr., Gerard, and others. 1994. *Financial Reform: Theory and Practice.* Cambridge University Press.

Demirguc-Kunt, Asli, and Ross Levine. 1996. "Stock Markets, Corporate Finance, and Economic Growth: Overview." *World Bank Economic Review* 10 (May): 223–39.

Fry, Maxwell J. 1988. *Money, Interest, and Banking in Economic Development.* Johns Hopkins University Press.

Goldsmith, Raymond W. 1969. *Financial Structure and Development.* Yale University Press.

Greenwood, Jeremy, and Bruce Smith. Forthcoming. "Financial Markets in Development, and the Development of Financial Markets." *Journal of Economic Dynamics and Control.*

King, Robert G., and Ross Levine. 1993a. "Finance and Growth: Schumpeter Might Be Right." *Quarterly Journal of Economics* 108 (August): 717–38.

———. 1993b. "Finance, Entrepreneurship, and Growth: Theory and Evidence." *Journal of Monetary Economics* 32 (December): 513–42.

Levine, Ross. 1991. "Stock Markets, Growth, and Tax Policy." *Journal of Finance* 46 (September): 1445–65.

Levine, Ross, and Sara Zervos. 1996. "Stock Market Development and Long-Run Economic Growth." *World Bank Economic Review* 10 (May): 323–39.

McKinnon, Ronald I. 1973. *Money and Capital in Economic Development.* Brookings.

Obstfeld, Maurice. Forthcoming. "Risk-Taking, Global Diversification, and Growth." *American Economic Review.*

Roubini, Nouriel, and Xavier Sala-I-Martin. 1992. "Financial Repression and Economic Growth." *Journal of Development Economics* 3(9): 5–50.

Schumpeter, Joseph A. 1912 (1932 edition). *The Theory of Economic Development,* translated by Redvers Opie. Harvard University Press.

Shaw, Edward S. 1973. *Financial Deepening in Economic Development.* Oxford University Press.

Stern, Nicholas. 1989. "The Economics of Development: A Survey." *Economics Journal* 99 (September): 597–685.

Vittas, Dimitri, ed. 1992. *Financial Regulation: Changing the Rules of the Game.* Washington: World Bank.

NOTES

1. Demirguc-Kunt and Levine (1996).

2. See Schumpeter (1912/1932); Cameron and others (1967); Goldsmith (1969); Shaw (1973); McKinnon (1973); Fry (1988).

3. Stern (1989).

4. King and Levine (1993a, 1993b).

5. In King and Levine (1993a, 1993b) we also study the ratio of deposit money bank domestic assets divided by deposit money bank domestic assets plus central bank domestic assets. This measure attempts to isolate which intermediaries—central banks or deposit money banks—are doing the intermediation. Banks probably provide better intermediary services than central banks so that this measure should be—and is—positively associated with economic growth.

In this study we also analyze 1) the ratio of credit issued to private enterprises divided by credit issues to central and local governments plus credit issued to public and private enterprises, and 2) the ratio of credit issued to private enterprises divided by GDP. Financial systems that primarily funnel credit to public enterprises and government probably provided fewer financial services than financial systems that allocate credit to private firms. These two measures are also positively and significantly associated with long-run growth.

6. This measure equals "$M3$" or line 551 from the International Financial Statistics; or when 551 is not available, we use line 34 plus line 35, which equals "$M2$."

7. King and Levine (1993b).

8. Goldsmith (1969).

9. Demirguc-Kunt and Levine (1996).

10. Bencivenga and Smith (1991); Levine (1991); Obstfeld (forthcoming).

11. King and Levine (1993b).

12. Bagehot (1873/1962, p. 53).

13. Greenwood and Smith (forthcoming).

14. Bagehot (1873/1962, pp. 3–4).

15. Levine (1991); Levine and Zervos (1996).

16. Roubini and Sala-I-Martin (1992); Bencivenga and Smith (1992).

17. See the article by Schiantarelli and others in Caprio and others (1994).

18. Caprio and others (1994); Vittas (1992); Brock (1992).

Chapter 3

R. BARRY JOHNSTON

The Speed of Financial Sector Reform: Risks and Strategies

Although the objectives and benefits of financial sector reform are well known, how to approach the transition from a repressed to a market-oriented financial system is still open to debate. Emphasizing the risks of financial sector reform, the conventional academic view has tended to place financial sector reform relatively late in the overall reform sequence and to favor a gradualist approach.[1] However, there are also arguments for following a more rapid approach to financial sector reform, which I address in this chapter.

Gradualism normally involves waiting to see the outcome of the previous reforms before embarking on the next steps; more rapid approaches usually involve reforming a number of areas simultaneously. The transition to a more market-oriented financial system also raises a number of issues for both macroeconomic and microeconomic policies. There are critical macroeconomic questions in designing financial sector reforms. What are the consequences of maintaining financial repression for economic performance—economic growth, inflation, and the balance of payments? Will it be possible to address poor economic performance, or to avoid the creation of inflation or balance of payments problems as part of a relatively rapid approach to financial sector reform? Will it be possible as part of this process to avoid serious overshooting in the level of interest rates and the exchange rate that could adversely affect the real sector? The main microeconomic concern relates to the capacity to address the weak institutional structure and market failures that are the legacy of prolonged financial repression, and that could result in poor resource allocation and a possible banking crisis following the financial sector reforms.

In this chapter I examine some of the macroeconomic and microeconomic issues that policymakers need to be aware of and to prepare for in the transition from a repressed to a market-oriented financial system. An assessment of the costs of financial repression and the capacity to respond to the risks of liberalizing financial markets can determine what will be feasible or desirable in terms of the speed of the reforms. The argument for more rapid reforms is that there could be important benefits for investment and economic growth.

In the next section I discuss monetary policy, and in the following section I review the fiscal implications of financial sector reform. I then review the coordination of financial sector reforms with the opening of the capital account of the balance of payments, followed by a discussion of the sources of institutional and market failures leading to microeconomic concerns with financial sector reform. Finally, I review considerations that would lead a country to follow a more rapid rather than a gradual approach to financial sector reform and offer some concluding remarks.

MONETARY CONTROL ISSUES

Many countries with repressed financial systems face problems of monetary control associated with the ineffectiveness of direct credit and interest rate controls. The problem with direct controls is not that the aggregates are uncontrollable; rather it is that because of circumvention and disintermediation, the controlled aggregates cease to bear a close relationship to the objectives of policy. The modification of monetary instruments to achieve more effective monetary control is an important motivation of financial sector reform, and the freeing of direct controls on interest rates and credit are central elements of most such reforms. Monetary control can be enhanced by increasing the reliance on indirect monetary instruments. These instruments include such open-market operations as auctions of government treasury bills or of central bank refinance credits or certificates of deposit to control money market liquidity.[2] Such instruments can provide the flexibility of open-market operations and a channel for the central bank to maintain monetary control during the initial phase of financial deregulation when markets are poorly developed. Increasing reliance on indirect monetary controls allows the authorities to eliminate the monetary regulatory distortions, including interest rate and credit controls, and a reliance on high non–interest-bearing reserve requirements that increase deposit-lending margins. Open market–type operations can also be catalytic in the development of domestic financial markets. It is therefore desirable to introduce these instruments very early in the financial sector reforms and to increase reliance on them to achieve monetary objectives.[3]

The elimination of credit and interest controls has also potentially important effects on monetary and credit aggregates, which have to be taken into account if a transition is to be successful. The liberalization of direct controls on credit and interest rates will likely be followed by an initial shift in the holdings of money and credit aggregates, as well as a structural change in the interest elasticity of their demand. The liberalization of controls on bank credit is often associated with large increases in the stocks of gross financial assets and liabilities, and borrowing to hold larger money balances. A liberation of bank interest rates may result in an initial rise in deposit rates relative to other rates of return and an increase in broad money holdings. Broad money may become less sensitive to changes in the general level of interest rates, because interest rates on bank deposits would move in line with competing interest rates. As a result of these structural shifts, the information content of broad monetary and credit aggregates will become difficult to assess during the transition phase; these aggregates will also become hard to control through changes in interest rates. As a result, authorities need to develop information systems to assess monetary conditions. Policy should be based on a review of a wider range of financial indicators—broad and narrow money, credit growth, inflation, and so on.

Given the potential shifts in asset demands, a greater focus may be placed on targeting real interest rates or the exchange rate, or on giving greater weight to these variables in the assessment of monetary conditions. However, the measurement of real interest rates creates a number of practical difficulties.[4] Experience also suggests that the information content and the stability of demand for the currency issue are usually less affected than the broader monetary aggregates by financial sector reform. This could argue for setting the intermediate and operating targets at the level of the central bank's balance sheet rather than the banking system.[5]

The elimination of direct controls on credit is often associated with a period during which credit to the private sector expands more rapidly than private sector deposits, as banks run down holdings of excess reserves and lower remunerated public sector assets accumulated during the period of credit controls. The more rapid growth of credit relative to deposits reflects a stock adjustment in the credit supply that will be temporary where the countries maintain positive real interest rates.[6] Nevertheless, credit expansion could result in a loss of macroeconomic control, adding to inflation or putting pressure on the balance of payments.

However, to attempt to control the temporary credit expansion through interest rates and indirect monetary controls could result in a potentially large increase in interest rates and appreciate the exchange rate, adversely affecting the real sector. The question is whether the stock adjustment should be phased as part of a gradual approach to the elimination of the credit controls or accommodated; and if it is accommodated, whether the potentially adverse macroeconomic effects can be avoided through a larger fiscal adjustment or through foreign inflows to protect the foreign exchange reserves. A phased approach could include allowing banks to increase credit only in response to increases in deposits. The credit controls should be supported by adjustments in interest rates and the indirect instruments of monetary policy. As I discuss in subsequent sections, the scope for generating a sufficient fiscal adjustment as part of a more rapid reform strategy is likely to be limited by the impact of the financial reforms on the fiscal deficit. Therefore, the rapid strategy may depend on generating simultaneous foreign inflows. This in turn depends on the early elimination of controls on the capital account of the balance of payments to help encourage a return of flight capital.

FISCAL IMPLICATIONS

Financial reforms render the magnitude of the fiscal imbalance transparent. Under financial repression, the actual fiscal burden is often hidden by the below-market rates of interest on government debt associated with compulsory purchases of debt by financial institutions, the use of an appreciated exchange rate for official transactions, and the costs borne by the central bank through subsidized lending, as well as among commercial banks through the accumulation of loan losses on publicly sponsored but loss-making projects.

These hidden deficits still impose a financial burden on the economy no less great for the fact that they are not shown in the fiscal accounts. The costs to the economy include low savings mobilization, capital flight, and resource misallocation associated with credit rationing, directed credits, and an appreciated and uncompetitive official exchange rate. Countries experiencing significant hidden fiscal costs need to undertake fiscal adjustment. Following the financial reforms, the measured budget deficit may be increased by liberalization of interest rates on government debt instruments, transfer to the budget of the costs of subsidized lending, the costs of restructuring the banking system, and the application of unified exchange rates to official transactions (although tax revenue may also be boosted by the adoption of a more realistic exchange rate). However, the capacity to finance the fiscal deficit can also be improved by the financial reforms because of new markets in government debt instruments and improved overall savings mobilization. The financial liberalization can also help to impose discipline on fiscal policy, because the newly emerging financial markets will send signals on the quality of fiscal policy and the need for fiscal action. In this way, governments may choose to deregulate financial markets—domestic and external—to constrain their own future decisions. In terms of efficiency of resource allocation, financial sector reforms will apply equally to either a large or small fiscal deficit.

Should financial sector reforms be delayed by the size of the fiscal deficit, as suggested by the sequencing literature? One reason suggested for delay is the potential loss of macroeconomic control. The risk is that without fiscal consolidation, the authorities would resort to money creation to cover the larger budget deficit. This comes back to the question of how to conduct monetary policy during the transition period, and the consequent need to develop indirect monetary instruments (including primary issue markets) for government debt and appropriate indicators to interpret monetary conditions. More generally, if the authorities are not committed to controlling the fiscal balance, the scope to maintain monetary control—whether through direct or indirect monetary controls—will be highly constrained.

Therefore, appropriate fiscal policy will be an important component of any program of economic or financial sector reform. In the case of liberal financial systems, the prospective fiscal deficit will be a major factor determining long-term interest rates. Under a repressed system, the prospective fiscal deficit will be a major factor determining the degree of financial repression.

There is a second possible reason for delaying financial sector reforms until necessary fiscal adjustments have been implemented. If the authorities avoid monetizing the deficit and finance it through market instruments, domestic interest rates could rise to high real levels. The exchange rate will then appreciate, increasing the adjustment burden on the real sector. This is of particular concern if the deficit is large, if financial markets are poorly developed, and if there is a lack of confidence in government policy.

But there are also counterarguments. Lack of confidence in government policy is a reason why fiscal consolidation should *accompany* financial sector reform but not be a reason for delaying such reforms until fiscal adjustment is completed. In addition, the concern that underdeveloped financial markets may make it difficult to finance the increased deficit does not appear warranted by experience. Countries have had some success in developing primary issue markets early in their financial sector reforms. Egypt's success in developing its treasury bill auctions is noteworthy in this regard. The initial underdevelopment of the capital market quite often merely reflects the government's unwillingness to pay market interest rates on its debt. Large fiscal deficits financed through financial repression also impose resource costs that must be taken into account and offset against the cost of raising interest rates in a deregulated environment.

Fiscal policy may also have other consequences for the effectiveness of financial sector reforms, and vice versa. For example, the tax deductibility of interest payments can blunt the effectiveness of interest rates as an instrument of monetary control. The tax structure may provide unwarranted incentives to borrow through one instrument rather than another or externally rather than domestically. Moreover, the loss of revenue from the reduction of high non–interest-bearing reserve requirements on banks may require compensating tax reforms.

LIBERALIZATION OF THE CAPITAL ACCOUNT

The liberalization of current external transactions and the adoption of market-determined exchange rate arrangements early in the reform process are widely accepted elements of a strategy of economic and financial sector reform. Recently there has been a greater focus on the complementary role of the liberalization of the capital account as part of the process of financial sector reform. The powerful effect that external financial liberalization can have in achieving a higher level of competition in the domestic financial system has been noted.[7] Empirical research has also increasingly pointed to the ineffectiveness of controls on capital movements in protecting developing countries' balance of payments and called into question the rationale for maintaining such controls.[8] There are a number of reasons why it may be desirable to undertake a more rapid liberalization of the capital account along with the reform of the domestic financial system.

—Because of the circumvention of controls and the existence of "black" foreign exchange markets, the degree of currency convertibility is already de facto high. The maintenance of capital controls serves mainly to result in pronounced statistical discrepancies in the balance of payments. This complicates the interpretation of underlying economic trends and obscures the interrelationship between domestic and external financial conditions.

—Freedom of international capital movements reinforces the policies to liberalize domestic interest rates and helps to create an environment conducive to a competitive and efficient domestic financial system. The institutional reforms needed to create efficient money and foreign exchange markets can be mutually supporting.

—Capital account liberalization in the context of appropriate macroeconomic policies contributes to a return of capital flight and supports the balance of payments during the period of domestic financial liberation. As I have noted, the liberalization of the domestic financial system can result in a rapid credit expansion that would tend to weaken the balance of payments and increase the measured fiscal deficit. Liberalizing the capital account to coincide with the domestic financial reforms, and the elimination of credit controls, may be instrumental in achieving a more rapid lifting of credit ceilings. The liberalization takes place against the background of reasonable confidence in government financial policies, or (if such confidence does not already exist) through accompanying fiscal consolidation.

Nevertheless, there are risks for the capital account from an inappropriate sequencing of reforms. A continued reliance on credit controls or high non–interest-bearing reserve requirements for monetary control purposes, or a failure to address inefficiencies in the domestic financial system, could lead to wide spreads between deposit and lending rates and encourage borrowing abroad rather than domestically. Such developments could result in an overvalued exchange rate and excessive external debt burden. Surges in capital inflows have become a problem in some countries.[9] Direct controls on credit and interest rates would be circumvented through the capital account. It would therefore be desirable to eliminate, as far as possible, the institutional and regulatory incentives to borrow abroad rather than domestically through an early reliance on indirect monetary controls. Domestic financial institutions and markets should be strengthened as part of a strategy of simultaneous liberalization of the capital account and the domestic financial system.

MICROECONOMIC CONCERNS

The major microeconomic concern with financial sector reform relates to the various sources of market failures or institutional weaknesses that are the legacy of prolonged financial repression. Market failures and resource misallocation are important problems of repressed financial systems. However, there is a risk that such developments will take different forms with financial liberalization, reducing the benefits for economic performance of the financial sector reforms. Financial sector reforms, especially rapid ones, have often been followed by financial crises.[10] Such crises have disrupted the financial sector, led to a contraction of income, and resulted in a temporary reversal of the financial deepening and the reforms. Financial crises can usually be traced to different country-specific characteristics, including weak bank supervision, lending to interrelated entities, problems of moral hazard, and inappropriate macroeconomic policies. But regardless of the specific cause of the crisis, the reforms often revealed major structural weaknesses in the financial sector. Banking solvency, for example, is quite often an issue at the commencement of financial sector reforms, reflecting the weak capital bases, poor loan portfolio, and inefficient management that existed during financial repression. The insolvent banks had incentives to allocate credit to high risk–high return projects without regard to the prospects for loan recovery, in an attempt to regain losses with the liberalization of balance sheet controls.

Another frequent problem has been interrelated ownership or incentive structures of banks and borrowers associated with lending to a few large enterprises in the old repressed financial systems involving credit rationing. Following financial reforms, increased lending to the interrelated enterprises can magnify risk exposures and reduce the supply of credit to new borrowers. Inefficient financial institutions that lack a commercial approach to banking emerge because of protection from competition under financial repression. Such institutions have high operating costs and lending margins and low deposit mobilization.

Other problems that came to the fore are unequal regulatory structures that have tolerated the existence of unregulated nonbanking institutions. These in turn have expanded as a result of direct controls on banks and have allocated credit for high-risk projects without due regard to prudential standards and inadequate accounting and information systems. The introduction of new freedoms to operate with financial reform can expose weaknesses in existing internal controls. Insufficiently diversified and developed financial markets, including foreign exchange markets, have been characteristic features under financial repression. The absence of such markets results in excessive concentrations of risk in the banking system, exposing borrowers to excessive interest rate risks or limitations on access to funds. Moral hazard resulting from explicit or implicit public sector guarantees, including many deposit insurance schemes, has been a problem resulting in the public's paying insufficient attention to the risks of different types of financial institutions. This was particularly a concern where such guarantees extended to unregulated nonbanking institutions or where they did not involve adequate, prudential regulation of the banks. Moral hazard problems also arise where banks and borrowers had low net worth, with weak incentives to internalize the consequences of their actions.

When a country liberalizes its financial sector, it may also become apparent that there are inadequate institutional capacities, knowledge, and skills (including among the central banks) to implement monetary control and appropriate supervision and regulation in a deregulated environment, and among financial institutions to assess and control risks. Poorly developed payment systems may provide inadequate incentives for efficient monetary management, thereby blunting the importance of interest rates in allocating resources.[11] Finally, rapid credit expansion in the wake of financial liberation can strain credit approval procedures, resulting in increased lending to risky projects.

These weaknesses need to be dealt with as part of the transition to a market orientation. In some countries, financial crises may have been necessary to promote a consensus on the need for action on restructuring the banking system and to overturn entrenched vested interests. A banking crisis in Russia helped destroy the old state banking system and consolidate the new banks' position. However, such an approach will likely be less than optimal for many countries, given the potential disruptive effect of a banking crisis and the risk that it will result in a reversal of financial sector reforms. A minimal system of bank supervision and regulation can help reduce the risk of financial crises and also improve the credit allocation processes. This should be an integral part of the strategy when embarking on financial sector reforms. Experience with banking crises suggests that the immediate focus should be on capital adequacy, lending to interrelated entities, large loan concentrations, loan classification and provisioning procedures, moral hazard, and the capacity for bank supervision both off and on site.[12] Concerning the unregulated nonbanking institutions, the best approach may be to allow those institutions that are insolvent to fail, and to require that solvent institutions meet minimum prudential standards in order to move toward a more level playing field for the regulation of financial transactions.

Technical assistance by national and international agencies can also assist the national authorities' efforts in addressing some of the structural and institutional weaknesses that lead to resource misallocation.[13] This assistance is provided at a number of levels: diagnostic and technical assistance missions, assignment of experts for hands-on assistance, staff training, and grants and loans for the acquisition of equipment and hardware to upgrade the financial system. The International Monetary Fund (IMF) assistance has focused on designing the monetary, exchange, and payment systems; developing the appropriate legal and regulatory arrangements, including central bank, commercial bank, and foreign exchange laws; and building the institutional capacity of the central banks, including those in monetary and exchange operations, bank supervisory functions, and payments systems. The IMF also works closely with other agencies to coordinate technical assistance in financial sector reform.[14]

CHOOSING BETWEEN RAPID AND GRADUAL LIBERALIZATION

Given the costs and risks of financial liberalization, what considerations might lead a country to follow a rapid (or a more gradual) approach to financial reform?

First, there is the question of whether the country can "afford" a gradualist approach that involves retaining elements of financial repression for long periods of time. The objective of financial reform is to improve the mobilization of financial resources and to achieve greater efficiency in their allocation. To postpone financial reform involves a potential high cost for economic growth. Typically, more gradualist approaches to reform have been followed in countries with high savings ratios—Japan and Korea, for example. Perhaps these countries could in some sense afford gradualism. Efficient financial systems were not critical to their domestic savings mobilization, and these countries could achieve high rates of growth even with some marginal inefficiency in resource allocation. More rapid financial liberalizations have been adopted by countries with low domestic savings rates as part of growth-oriented strategies, such as in some of the South American countries. The objectives of these reforms are not only to increase savings mobilization, but also to allocate it more efficiently.

There is also the question of the de facto (as opposed to the official) economy. Parallel, market-oriented financial institutions and markets evolve even in the most highly regulated of economies. Direct credit and interest rate controls result in disintermediation and the growth of curb markets; exchange controls are circumvented through various channels, including the under- and overinvoicing of foreign trade transactions. When the incentives that encourage the shadow economy are large, the economy's official sector may come to represent only a fraction of total economic activity. Such an outcome is quite often observed in war-torn economies or in countries that have been through major political upheavals. In designing the appropriate strategy for reform, national authorities should recognize the de facto nature of the economy to frame an effective strategy in regaining macroeconomic control. A useful move, for example, will often be to quickly eliminate the constraints on the official sector and to rely on markets and indirect controls that affect the formal and informal sectors more equally.

There are also important broad issues of political economy. In some cases, rapid financial liberalizations have been used as the catalyst to broad economic reform and as a way of overcoming inertia in certain parts of the economy, such as the labor market. It is usually easier politically to start reforms in the financial sector rather than other areas. More rapid reforms may be needed to overcome entrenched interests. Moreover, rapid reforms can add credibility to a government's commitment to carry out reform, thereby helping in the mobilization of external resources. Speed shows tangible evidence that the authorities are moving ahead with reforms and the evident willingness of the government to subject itself to market discipline. Some of these factors were important in New Zealand's decision to rapidly liberalize both its domestic financial system and external transactions in 1984–85.

Finally, financial sector reforms are often undertaken in complex economic and political circumstances. In many cases the reforms are an essential part of programs of macroeconomic stabilization, which became necessary because of the failure of a repressed financial system to deliver adequate economic performance. Countries may not have the luxury of stabilizing or of creating the desirable institutional preconditions before embarking on financial sector reform; stabilization and reform have to be pursued together. Gradual approaches to reform may also impose larger burdens of implementation on policymakers than more decisive action would. The strategies and approaches to financial sector reform must weigh all of these factors carefully.

CONCLUSIONS

There is a cluster of issues connected with the concept of sequencing. The literature on sequencing has tended to place financial sector reforms relatively late in the overall reform process. Typically, a gradualist approach is favored. However, if the costs of maintaining financial controls are taken into account (for example, low savings mobilization, capital flight, lack of monetary control, and an inefficient allocation of resources), a strategy of more rapid financial sector reform appears likely to achieve better economic performance. The risks of rapid reform can be anticipated and prepared for.

A more rapid strategy would involve early adoption of market-based monetary controls, simultaneous liberalizations of the domestic financial system and the capital account of the balance of payments, and concurrent fiscal consolidation and strengthening of financial institutions and markets. Key monetary control reforms, including the introduction of indirect controls (such as open-market operations), should be initiated early in the reform process. Such a requirement reflects the critical objectives of achieving control while allowing for the removal of various discriminatory controls on interest rates, credit, and financial institution portfolios. The elimination of domestic financial distortions and the simultaneous liberalization of the controls on capital movements could be mutually reinforcing by increasing competition and encouraging a return of flight capital. Concurrent fiscal adjustment would be essential to enhance credibility, reduce pressure on market interest rates, and support monetary policy in the deregulated environment. Institution building, regulatory reform, and a minimum system of prudential regulation would thus be critical elements in the overall reform strategy, allowing the country to borrow abroad (which may be another key objective). Lack of a credible fiscal policy and failure to address banking sector problems would run the risk of reversing the whole reform effort early on.

REFERENCES

Baliño, Tomàs J. T., Juhi Dhawan, and V. Sundararajan. 1994. "Payments System Reforms and Monetary Policy in Emerging Market Economies in Central and Eastern Europe." IMF Staff Papers 41(3) (September): 383–410.

Bisat, Amer, R. Barry Johnston, and V. Sundararajan. 1992. "Issues in Managing and Sequencing Financial Sector Reforms: Lessons from Experiences in Five Developing Countries." Working Paper WP/92/82. Washington: International Monetary Fund (October).

Guitiàn, Manuel. 1994. "The Role of Financial Sector Reform in Macroeconomic and Structural Adjustment." Paper prepared for seminar, "Financial Policies and Capital Markets In Arab Countries." Abu Dhabi, United Arab Emirates. January 25.

Johnston, R. Barry. 1991. "Sequencing Financial Reforms." In *The Evolving Roles of Central Banks*, edited by Patrick Downes and Reza Vaez-Zadeh, 295–306. Washington: International Monetary Fund.

_____. 1993. "Aspects of the Design of Financial Programs with the Adoption of Indirect Monetary Controls." Paper on Policy Analysis and Assessment PPAA/93/16. Washington: International Monetary Fund (October).

Johnston, R. Barry, and Odd Per Brekk. 1989. "Monetary Control Procedures and Financial Reform: Approaches, Issues and Recent Experiences in Developing Countries." Working Paper WP/89/48. Washington: International Monetary Fund (June).

Johnston, R. Barry, and Chris Ryan. 1994. "The Impact of Controls on the Private Capital Accounts of Countries' Balance of Payments: Empirical Estimates and Policy Implications." Working Paper WP/94/78. Washington: International Monetary Fund (July).

McKinnon, Ronald I. 1991. *The Order of Economic Liberalization: Financial Control in the Transition to a Market Economy*. Johns Hopkins University Press.

Schadler, Susan, and others. 1993. "Recent Experiences with Surges in Capital Inflows." Occasional Paper 108. Washington: International Monetary Fund.

Zulu, J. B. 1994. "MAE Activities Expand in Response to Calls for Technical Assistance, Global Conditions." *IMF Survey* (May).

NOTES

1. The "conventional" approach suggests that fiscal adjustment should occur before financial sector liberalization and the elimination of controls on capital movements should occur after the domestic financial system is liberalized. See, for example, McKinnon (1991).

2. For a discussion of monetary control procedures and financial sector reforms, see Johnston and Brekk (1989).

3. Some countries temporarily maintain certain types of direct credit controls until the intended degree of monetary restraint has been achieved

through indirect instruments. However, the maintenance of the direct control may result in continued resource misallocation.

4. These difficulties include the measurement of inflation expectations, and the choice of the appropriate interest rate or price index and thus the real interest rate will vary depending on the agent involved, and the need to take tax rates into account.

5. These issues and alternative approaches to monetary control that can be adopted during the period of financial sector reform are discussed in Johnston (1993).

6. For an analysis of country experience leading to these conclusions, see Bisat, Johnston, and Sundararajan (1992).

7. See Guitiàn (1994).

8. An examination of the impact of exchange controls on the private capital accounts of countries' balance of payments using cross country data for the period 1985–92 indicated that these controls had no significant impact on developing countries' balance of payments. There was some weak evidence that the elimination of exchange control actually improved the balance of payments. See Johnston and Ryan (1994).

9. See Schadler and others (1993).

10. See Bisat, Johnston, and Sundararajan (1992).

11. The importance of payments system reform as part of financial sector reforms is discussed in Baliño, Dhawan, and Sundararajan (1994).

12. Johnston (1991).

13. The International Monetary Fund (IMF), the World Bank, and national agencies, including the U.S. Agency for International Development (USAID), are important providers of technical assistance in the area of financial sector reform.

14. See Zulu (1994) for a discussion of the IMF's Monetary and Exchange Affairs Department role in providing and coordinating technical assistance in the area of financial sector reform.

Chapter 4

DAVID C. COLE

Sequencing versus Practical Problem Solving in Financial Sector Reform

The literature on sequencing of financial reforms has focused on broad policy changes and suggested that certain of these changes should precede others, or certain changes should be deferred until others have been implemented if serious adverse outcomes are to be avoided. The early recommendations from Shaw, quoting himself and McKinnon, were to do everything at once.[1] When this prescription was tried in the Southern Cone countries of Latin America in the late 1970s, it did in fact have seriously adverse consequences. This led to the new literature on sequencing, including work by Edwards and McKinnon, among others.[2] Although they may have differed on some points, these two authors, along with Dornbusch and Reynoso, were united in proposing that the capital account should be the last major policy area to be decontrolled.[3] If the capital account were decontrolled prematurely, before other financial and trade policies had been shifted to a market-determined basis, they predicted that not only would investment allocation be less efficient, but the capital account could and would also experience extreme swings. Such swings would be impossible to control by market-based instruments. This in turn would seriously disrupt the economy, as it had in the Southern Cone.[4]

Literature that takes a contrary view has recently appeared. It suggests that decontrolling the capital account may be an appropriate move early in the reform process. This will impose a discipline on other aspects of macroeconomic policy that will help maintain overall stability and, in turn, contribute generally to development.[5]

The most widely recognized example of this "reverse" sequencing is Indonesia. This nation completely decontrolled its capital account in

47

1970 and maintained that policy continuously thereafter—despite booms and collapses of oil revenues, episodes of tightening and loosening of trade controls and domestic financial controls, and inflows and outflows of foreign capital. Assessments in recent years have all emphasized how the early opening of the capital account in Indonesia helped to maintain fiscal discipline and force corrective adjustments in other areas of macroeconomic policy in response to signals from the capital account.[6]

In this chapter I argue that theoretical propositions about or empirical searches for optimal sequences for macroeconomic policy reforms will likely prove unrewarding. In fact, they can actually be counterproductive if they suggest to policymakers that carrying out an important macroeconomic policy reform is inappropriate if some other macroeconomic policy change has not already been implemented. Economic policymaking, especially in developing countries, can be a highly opportunistic process. If a situation arises that focuses attention on a fundamental problem and policymakers are looking for a solution, it would be the height of folly to suggest that the necessary corrective action could not be taken because it would be out of sequence. The obvious solution for the practical politician is to put together a package of policies and measures that address the problem. The combining of reinforcing actions to focus on particular needs in light of prevailing circumstances is what policy advisors should focus on, rather than some mystical notion of optimal policy sequencing.

Often the enactment of one major policy measure creates or clarifies the need for others. This is a kind of sequencing, but it is the reverse of the usual steps. For example, the conventional sequential recommendation would be to put a system of prudential regulations in place before opening up the capital markets. But it may be difficult to get policymakers to focus on the need for such regulations before the decontrolling measures are put into effect. If an elaborate set of prudential regulations is first put in place, it may also deter new interest in the ostensibly decontrolled market, especially by the more speculative investors. Similarly, the conventional sequential recommendation would be to develop effective market-based monetary policy instruments before removing direct controls over bank credit. But it is difficult to generate interest in (much less experiment with) market-based monetary instruments if there is no apparent need and no active market in which to try out the potential instruments.

Both of these examples reflect Indonesian experience. The Indonesian government removed direct controls over bank lending in June 1983 and then began to experiment with various market-based instruments of monetary policy in early 1984. This experimentation has continued for over a decade; meanwhile, the central bank has gradually grown more accepting of market-determined (rather than directly controlled) interest rates for money market instruments. Similarly, the Indonesian capital markets were actively promoted by the nation's government in 1988–89 before adoption of a comprehensive set of prudential regulations in December 1990. This sequencing inevitably resulted in some new issues coming into the market without adequate disclosure. As a result, certain enthusiastic early buyers experienced sizable losses. But it was these kinds of problems that focused the minds of the responsible government officials on the need for better prudential regulation, which soon led to the adoption of new rules and a strengthening of the regulatory agency.

A much more important but largely neglected aspect of sequencing is the institutional or structural dimensions of the financial system.[7] Shaw put major emphasis on development of the banking system. He was scathing in his critique of attempts to introduce long-term financial institutions or capital markets either prematurely or as an alternative to a repressed and ineffective banking system.[8] Nevertheless, many countries in Africa as well as former socialist countries are being pressured to set up elaborate money and capital markets. This pressure builds up despite the deficiencies of their banking and payments systems, not to mention the other elements of infrastructure needed to make such markets competitive and efficient. This perverse sequencing of financial structure evolution may provide short-term rewards for foreign technicians and information system hucksters. However, it is likely to prove costly in the longer run for the countries in question, in terms of both growth and stability.

MACROECONOMIC VERSUS MICROECONOMIC POLICY SEQUENCING

It is useful to make the distinction between macroeconomic policy sequencing on the one hand and microeconomic policy and institutional sequencing on the other. Macroeconomic policies in this context refer to the basic fiscal, monetary, foreign exchange, or trade policy regimes of a country; whether the fiscal policy stance is prone to deficits, surpluses or neutral; whether monetary policy is implemented through market-based instruments or through direct controls; and whether it is expansionary or contractionary. In contrast, microeconomic policies are used here as subsets of the broader macroeconomic policies. If exogenous forces cause a disturbance in the macroeconomic balance, microeconomic policy instruments can be used to help restore it. If a basic macroeconomic policy change is introduced, such as removal of foreign exchange controls, microeconomic policy instruments can be brought into play to reinforce the macroeconomic change, or to dampen possible destabilizing or other undesirable consequences. Microeconomic policies imply a kind of fine-tuning of the macroeconomic changes. Similarly, institutional changes refer to adjustments in legislation (laws, regulations, rules, and the like) or procedures, performance standards, or even leadership and staffing of organizations that have a bearing on the implementation of economic policies.

Changes in basic macroeconomic policies are generally difficult to bring about. They are often preceded by a change in national leadership or by an economic crisis that disrupts the whole economy and raises questions about the suitability of previous macroeconomic policies.[9] When such events occur, and when such opportunities present themselves, they should be acted upon. Often the most crucial macroeconomic policy change will be related to circumstances that have precipitated the political change or the economic crisis. Changes in microeconomic policies are easier to bring into effect. They generally do not require broad approval from many agencies or political bodies but can be implemented by a minister or central bank governor with the approval of the head of government. Institutional changes lie somewhere in between—especially if they call for any change in the way people behave, or learn and use new skills, or give up discretionary authority over remunerative economic activities.

The ability of a government to recognize the need for and then to implement changes in microeconomic policies or in institutions to deal with emerging problems can be critical to whether or not financial reforms succeed. If this ability is lacking, then it is quite likely that there will be overshooting and instability. A factor that obviously influences such outcomes is the political strength and cohesion of the government. A related concern is the willingness of key decisionmakers to be informed of emerging problems. In countries where leadership changes frequently, political power is often fragmented; but where leadership does not change for long periods, there is often a tendency to protect the leader from bad news and to let problems continue without seeking solutions for them. Another influencing factor is whether a major policy reform has been developed internally or imported or imposed from outside. If it is internally generated, then the expected consequences of major policy changes are probably better understood and the danger signals more likely to be noticed. But imported policy measures may be heading for trouble without the responsible officials knowing what to look for, much less how to respond.

A POLICY REGIME AND ENVIRONMENT MATRIX

I have suggested that there are many fundamental factors that bear on the macroeconomic policymaking process. It may be helpful to view these in a broad conceptual framework (table 4-1). The policy regimes and environments are broadly categorized as "restrictive," "intermediate," and "liberalized." The various areas of macroeconomic policy and policy environment are then similarly divided up according to these broad categories.

During their previous colonial existence, many developing countries had relatively liberal macroeconomic policy regimes, sustained by colonial legal and political systems and a reasonably capable financial system, all designed to serve the interests of the colonialists. After independence many countries, confronted with serious financial disturbances and their own limited capabilities for dealing with them, shifted to much more restrictive systems of both macroeconomic policy and governance. The economic and political development process that many poor countries now face involves a kind of migration from the more restrictive to the more liberalized systems, including the transformation of the environmental factors that strongly influence the feasibility of macroeconomic policies.

TABLE 4-1. *Policy Regimes and Environments*

Policy area or environment	Restrictive systems	Intermediate systems	Liberalized systems
MACROECONOMIC POLICY REGIMES			
Foreign exchange policy			
Capital account	Highly controlled	Semicontrolled	Open
Exchange rate	Fixed rigidly	Managed	Market-based
		—crawling peg	—with intervention
		—bands	—without intervention
Monetary policy			
Interest rates	Controlled	Guided	Market-based
Credit allocation	Rigidly controlled	Semicontrolled	Market-based
Instruments of monetary management	Central bank credit	Reserve requirements and direct control of reserve money	Effective open market operations
Fiscal policy	Uncontrolled deficits	Rigid balanced budget	Flexible budget balance
Trade policy	Strong protective restrictions	Mixed protection and export promotion	Marked-based, limited distortions
Prudential supervision	Direct oversight of credit allocation	Minimal supervision and oversight	Effective prudential supervision of asset quality
ENVIRONMENTAL FACTORS			
Legal system	Minimum effectiveness	Moderately effective	Fully effective
Political regime	Centralized controls, much corruption	Moderately open, moderate corruption	Open, effective regime, minimal corruption
Financial institution capability	Few, inefficient, oligopolistic	Moderately efficient and diversified	Open, competitive, and efficient

It is unrealistic to expect that there will normally be some sort of steady, across-the-board transition from restrictive systems to liberal ones. Different countries will find it appropriate, or expedient, to focus their efforts on certain areas within a given time frame and leave others until later. The theoretical advocates of macroeconomic policy sequencing are suggesting there is some appropriate hierarchy among these policy areas. The practical political economist understands the need to focus on the macroeconomic policy area that is currently causing the most harm to the economy, that is most amenable to improvement, or ideally, that is both critical and amenable to change.

Policy Regimes and Policy Changes in Indonesia

Table 4-2 applies this broad analytical framework to Indonesian experience between 1968 and 1988. In table 4-2, the two decades are divided into three periods, broadly characterized as liberalizing in 1968–72, more restrictive in 1973–82, and then liberalizing again in 1983–88. A more recent five-year period has two distinguishable periods, 1989–90 and 1991–93, each of which experienced both liberalizing and restrictive changes, thereby making an overall characterization more difficult (table 4-3).

In the first period, 1968–72, when the dominant objectives were stabilization and recovery, the Indonesian government took several important liberalizing steps. These included eliminating foreign capital controls and foreign exchange allocation systems, unifying the exchange rate and making the rupiah fully convertible, setting bank deposit interest rates at positive real levels, and balancing the fiscal budget. During the period 1973–82, which was marked by high oil revenues, many restrictive policies were imposed, but the open capital account and full currency convertibility were retained. Then in the third period, 1983–88, when oil prices declined, trade policy shifted to encouragement of nonoil exports along with continued protection of domestic industries, and new taxes were introduced to replace the lost oil revenues. In the financial area, during the third period major steps were taken to liberalize bank interest rates and loan allocation decisions, although central bank credit channeled through the state banks continued to play an important role.

Over these two decades, in terms of macroeconomic policy changes, there was first fiscal stabilization, followed by liberalization of the current and capital accounts, and imposition of positive real bank deposit interest rates. Then with high oil revenues came some loss of fiscal control, restrictive credit policies, negative real interest rates,

TABLE 4-2. *Indonesian Policy Regimes and Environments, 1968–88[a]*

Policy area or environment	1968–72	1973–82	1983–88
Capital account	**Moving from semicontrolled to open**	**Open outflow, some controls on inflows**	Open outflow, some controls on inflows
Exchange rate	**Evolved from dual to unified, market determined**	Rigidly fixed between devaluations	Rigidly fixed between devaluations
Monetary policy	Pervasive direct controls	*Increasing microcontrols*	**Much reduced direct control**
Interest rates	**Set by central bank, positive real rates**	*Set by central bank, negative real rates*	**Market-based**
Credit allocation	Influenced by central bank	*Ceilings and allocation by central bank*	**Mostly market-based, some loan subsidies by central bank**
Instruments of monetary management	Strong guidance by central bank	*Credit ceilings and interest rate controls*	**Limited open-market operations, direct transfers of government deposits**
Fiscal policy	**Moving toward rigid budget balance**	*Balanced regular budget, uncontrolled state enterprises*	**Balanced budget**
Trade policy	Relatively open, much smuggling	*Increasing protection of manufacturing*	**Shift to mixed protection and export promotion in 1986**
Prudential supervision	Central bank directed all aspects of state-owned banks	Same as previous period, but government-sponsored limited capital market	Limited supervision of increasingly important private banks

TABLE 4-2. *(Continued)*

Legal system	Very limited effectiveness, rely mainly on administrative authority	Same	Same
Political regime	Centralized controls, moderate corruption	*Centralized controls, increasing corruption and diffusion of power*	**Reduction of centralized controls over financial system and private firms**
Financial institution capability	Very limited, mainly state-owned banks dominated by central bank	Same as previous period	**Increasing capability and competition especially in private banks**

a. Bold type indicates liberalizing measures or changes. Italics indicate restrictive measures or changes.

and increased trade policy distortions. Finally, with the decline in oil revenues, new taxes were introduced, credit and interest controls were removed, and trade policy shifted toward promotion of nonoil exports. The legal and prudential environments gave little support to these changes in economic policies.

In the five-year period 1989–93, there was a mix of liberalizing and restrictive policies. Initially, in 1989–90, new policy measures that freed up entry into most areas of financial activity resulted in rapid expansion of institutions but without accompanying improvements in prudential supervision, raising concerns about the quality and soundness of the new institutions. Monetary policy was characterized by loss of control over monetary expansion but showed improvement in foreign exchange management, which helped to prevent large capital outflows. In response to concerns about both institutional solvency and possible capital outflows, tough new prudential regulations for the banking system and the capital markets were implemented in 1991–93, along with highly restrictive monetary policies. These restraints on domestic financial expansion pushed up domestic interest rates and encouraged large capital inflows. This in turn led to new restraints on incoming capital

TABLE 4-3. *Indonesian Policy Regimes and Environments, 1989–93*[a]

Policy area or environment	1989–90	1991–93
Capital account	**Fully open**	*Open, but with restrictions on inflows*
Exchange rate	**Crawling peg tied to U.S. dollar with narrow bands**	**Crawling peg tied to dollar plus inflation differential, wider bands**
Monetary policy	**No effective restraints on monetary expansion**	Strong restraints through prudential ratios
Interest rates	Central bank guidance of state bank rates	**No guidance on bank rates, mainly influenced by money market rates**
Credit allocation	**No controls on private banks, continued provision of subsidized credit to state banks**	**Major reduction in subsidized credits, no restrictions on other credit**
Instruments of monetary management	*No effective instruments, central bank set rates on its bills to guide banks*	**Increasingly effective open market operations based on central bank bills**
Fiscal policy	*Destabilizing management of government deposit balances*	**Flexible budget balance and coordination with central bank on government funds management**
Trade policy	Increasing export promotion with continuing protection	Same as previous period
Prudential supervision	**Free entry of banks and other financial institutions**, ineffective supervision of banks and capital markets	**Imposition of new prudential rules for banks and capital markets**
Legal system	Very limited effectiveness, rely mainly on administrative authority	**New laws and regulations provide basis for legal actions against fraud and mismanagement**
Political regime	*Centralized controls, moderate corruption, exploiting new financial liberalization*	*Centralized controls, increasing corruption and concentration of politicoeconomic power*

TABLE 4-3. *(Continued)*

Financial institution capability	Very rapid expansion of banks and capital market institutions and training of new personnel; active competition to provide new services	Cleaning up of bad loans/ investments and tightening up of internal controls to meet new prudential requirements and increased competition

a. Bold type indicates liberalizing measures or changes. Italics indicate restrictive measures or changes.

and increased discretionary controls over management of foreign financing. Stronger prudential supervision and legal foundations also improved the quality of domestic financial institutions.

This brief review of the changes in macroeconomic and financial policy regimes in Indonesia over the past quarter-century illustrates that, in the real world, policies do not normally evolve in a consistent, unidirectional manner—certainly not in response to some underlying sequential logic. Often powerful external forces (such as changes in world oil prices) may precipitate actions that will understandably be quite different in oil-exporting and oil-importing countries. Similarly, major macroeconomic policy changes will likely lead to a learning period and a number of follow-up measures intended to reinforce, or perhaps even undermine, the initial change. The art of good policymaking is to anticipate the need for follow-up measures before that need turns into a serious crisis, and then to recognize and (one hopes) prevent efforts to reverse the original reforms.

REFERENCES

Boediono. 1994. "Problems of Implementing Monetary Policy in Indonesia." In *Indonesia Assessment 1994*, edited by Ross H. McLeod. Canberra: Australian National University.
Chant, John, and Mari Pangestu. 1994. "An Assessment of Financial Reform in Indonesia, 1983–90." In *Financial Reform: Theory and Experience*, edited by Gerard Caprio, Jr., Izak Atiyas, and James A. Hanson, 223–75. Cambridge University Press.

Cole, David C., and Betty F. Slade. 1991. "Reform of Financial Systems." In *Reforming Economic Systems in Developing Countries*, edited by Dwight H. Perkins and Michael Roemer, 313–40. Harvard Institute for International Development.

———. 1992. "Financial Development in Indonesia." In *The Oil Boom and After: Indonesian Economic Policy and Performance in the Suharto Era*, edited by Anne Booth. Singapore: Oxford University Press.

———. 1993. "Indonesian Financial Development—A Different Sequencing?" In *Financial Sector Regulation: Changing the Rules of the Game*, edited by Dimitri Vittas. Washington: World Bank.

Diaz-Alejandro, Carlos. 1985. "Goodbye Financial Repression, Hello Financial Crash." *Journal of Development Economics* 19 (September/October): 1–24.

Dornbusch, Rudiger, and Alejandro Reynoso. 1989. "Financial Factors in Economic Development." *American Economic Review* 79 (May): 204–209.

Edwards, Sebastian. 1984. "The Order of Liberalization of the External Sector in Developing Countries." *Princeton Essays in International Finance* No. 156.

Hanson, James A. 1994. "An Open Capital Account: A Brief Survey of the Issues and the Results." In *Financial Reform: Theory and Experience*, edited by Gerard Caprio, Jr., Izak Atiyas, and James A. Hanson. Cambridge University Press.

McKinnon, Ronald I. 1982. "The Order of Economic Liberalization: Lessons from Chile and Argentina." In *Economic Policy in a World of Change*, edited by Karl Brunner and Allan Meltzer, 159–86. Amsterdam: North Holland.

———. 1989. "Macroeconomic Instability and Moral Hazard in a Liberalizing Economy." In *Latin American Debt and Adjustment: External Shocks and Macroeconomic Policies*, edited by Philip L. Brock, Michael Connolly, and Claudio Gonzalez-Vega, 99–111. Praeger, 1989.

———. 1991. *The Order of Economic Liberalization: Financial Control in the Transition to a Market Economy*. Johns Hopkins University Press.

Shaw, Edward S. 1973. *Financial Deepening in Economic Development*. Oxford University Press.

Wardhana, Ali. 1994. "Financial Reform: Achievements, Problems and Prospects." In *Indonesia Assessment 1994*, edited by Ross H. McLeod, 79–93. Canberra: Australian National University.

NOTES

1. Shaw (1973, p. 251).
2. Edwards (1984); McKinnon (1982; 1989; 1991).
3. Dornbusch and Reynoso (1989).

4. See Diaz-Alejandro (1985).

5. Hanson (1994) gives an up-to-date summary of the current literature.

6. Cole and Slade (1992; 1993); Wardhana (1994); Boediono (1994); Chant and Pangestu (1994).

7. Shaw (1973).

8. Shaw (1973, pp. 144–47).

9. Cole and Slade (1991).

Chapter 5

STEPHAN HAGGARD

The Political Economy of Financial Market Reform

In most discussions of financial market reform, economists and financial analysts seek to understand the economic consequences of reform and then make policy prescriptions to address those consequences. The purpose of my comments here, by contrast, is to offer some reflections on the political economy of financial market reform. What are the incentives facing the politicians and bureaucrats who make final decisions with respect to financial market policy? Under what conditions will governments initiate reform measures? What institutions are required to sustain them?

The political economy of financial markets in the advanced industrial states is generally an elite politics. In contrast to more broadly politicized economic issues, such as fiscal or trade policy, financial market policy involves a relatively small number of market players, industry associations, regulators, and (in the United States) legislators who represent the financial centers and thus have an electoral interest in the issue.

The small but growing literature on the politics of deregulation in advanced industrial states has emphasized the pressure to change existing domestic controls—whether capital controls, interest rate controls, or regulatory restrictions—that comes from the growing internationalization of financial markets. Typically, it is the more internationalized segments of both the financial and real sectors of the economy that come to view such domestic controls as a constraint and mobilize to reduce them. Capital account and interest rate controls can hinder international competitiveness—for example, by limiting the deposit and customer base (that is, by discouraging capital inflows and encouraging outflows seeking higher returns) or complicating foreign transactions or operations. These segments of the financial

60

sector are also most likely to be sensitive to external political pressures for reciprocity and market opening, particularly from the United States. The deregulation of Japan's financial markets exhibits evidence of both of these lines of external pressure.

External-pressure politics have also operated on a number of the more advanced developing countries that have sustained fairly strong economic performance, such as Korea and Taiwan. As in Japan, liberalization in both countries has been quite gradual, however. The conditions that make aggressive liberalization a more plausible strategy—namely, good aggregate performance, with its positive implications both for the balance of payments and for the net worth of borrowers—also produced fewer incentives to liberalize rapidly.

In most other developing and socialist countries, it is difficult to disentangle the politics of finance from the broader and more contentious politics of stabilization, structural adjustment, and transition to the market. Not surprisingly, fiscal crises, balance of payments problems, and financial setbacks have played a central role in triggering reform. Fiscal crises make it costly to sustain preferential credit programs that have high absolute and opportunity costs. Balance of payments difficulties usually result in the imposition of capital controls in the short run, but the quest for investment and the involvement of multilateral financial institutions both press in the opposite direction over time. Of course, banking crises were a ubiquitous concomitant of the economic difficulties of the 1980s and provided an even more immediate motive for rethinking past financial market policies.

The difference between the politics of reform in the advanced industrial states and the developing world is therefore quite striking. The process in the advanced industrial states is anchored by strong and concentrated interests that have supported and even led the liberalization process. In the developing countries, by contrast, liberalization and deregulation have often been launched under duress and are thus much more fragile and subject to reversal in the face of a recurrence of economic difficulties.

For this reason, the speed and sequencing of reform—a major theme of this book—are of political as well as economic interest. The debate about sequencing is ultimately about the complementarity or interdependence of different components of the overall reform process—or, to put it differently, whether there are positive, negative, or no externalities from one reform to another.

Choices about the steps and speed of sequencing are also premised on implicit models of political economy, however. There are three political arguments for rapid or telescoped reform. The first is that in any reform process, there will inevitably be adjustments and compromises required once a policy is initiated. When windows of opportunity arise as a result of a crisis or change in government, it is therefore important to exploit them fully. The second argument for rapid reform is that it may have substantial costs in the short run, but the faster the government acts, the faster the economy will go through the dislocation and distributive reshuffling associated with changing relative prices, and the sooner new bases of support will emerge. Finally, by moving rapidly, the government may actually help disorganize those stakeholders who are against reform. For example, tightening budget constraints or privatizing firms undercuts inefficient firms, which are the most important lobbyists for subsidized credit.

The Achilles' heel of these arguments for rapid reform centers on the credibility of the reform effort. If the configuration of interests is opposed to the reform or the costs of imposing it are great, then the reform is unlikely to stick, particularly in democratic settings. It is therefore better to work out compromises among the major players at the outset. Sequencing can thus be seen as a political strategy for building coalitions of support for the transition to a new policy equilibrium.

Who is likely to be part of these antireform interests? First are the recipients of subsidized credit. The findings from our studies of financial market reform in middle-income East Asian and Latin American countries suggest that this problem is less severe than one might expect.[1] Those with privileged access to subsidized finance are likely to be large groups reasonably well placed to adjust to a liberalized financial environment and even to profit from it by diversifying into new financial activities. The Korean chaebol provide an example.

The exception to this rule are the state-owned enterprises in both capitalist and transition economies, where the imposition of a hard budget constraint raises major political problems. A number of these firms are economically unviable, raising the question of whether they can withstand the pressures of liberalization, and if so at what cost.

But the fact of government ownership makes them particularly vulnerable to political protest, especially from employees, who fear the loss of jobs and income.

A second set of pressures comes from the banking, securities, and insurance industries. One problem is a straightforward issue of protection and barriers to entry to thwart competition. Foreign entry is likely to pose political problems, as domestic financial enterprises seek to resist the introduction of greater competition into the domestic market. Support for foreign entry is weakened because it lacks a domestic constituency. More important, the very regime of financial repression itself tends to create a particularly concentrated financial system in which a small number of financial enterprises are likely to be both economically and politically powerful; the Philippines provides a clear example. That repressive policy regime has also likely contributed to the weak balance sheets of the banks and an explosion of nonperforming assets. This weak financial position actually *enhances* the political leverage of the banking sector over the government. The result—visible in the financial sector agreement in the North American Free Trade Agreement (NAFTA) and in recent liberalization in Korea, as well as in banking deregulation in the United States—is to provide various protections for existing institutions to avoid confronting serious downsizing and the economic and social dislocations it can create.

I have proceeded on the assumption that rent seeking is the primary problem with financial reform. But this may be less of a problem than the rent-granters: the politicians and bureaucrats who profit from financial repression and external controls. Financial repression creates a good that can be distributed for political ends. In our comparative analysis, we found ubiquitous evidence of the use of financial instruments as a political tool for building bases of support. It must also be emphasized that the government itself benefits directly from controls by lowering its own cost of borrowing. Finance ministries may thus have mixed motives with respect to reform: favoring it on efficiency grounds, yet exhibiting reluctance because of its consequences for government finances.

I have already noted the role of crisis in overcoming these dilemmas and forcing the government's hand. But the key political question is not simply whether the government can initiate reforms but whether the reforms can be sustained. The main lacuna I see in the literature on financial market reform is not the question of what policies are optimal (though important disagreements remain on that score) but on what administrative structures and processes are likely to generate good, flexible policy over time. This is not simply an issue of building administrative capacity—that is, of "good government"—but of building institutions that align incentives of all involved parties in a pro-reform direction.

The first important lesson in this regard is the importance of delegating authority away from the executive and even the government toward independent agencies. Recent literature on central bank independence is germane, emphasizing the correlation between central bank independence and the stability of both monetary policy and inflation. Moreover, because the mandate of the central bank is centered on maintaining price stability, independent central banks are likely to take a skeptical view of financial market policies (such as preferential credit) that have adverse macroeconomic consequences, and to favor reforms (such as developing money, bond, and foreign exchange markets) that make their task easier.

It is interesting to note, however, that although measures of legal independence, such as the terms of appointment and removal of governors, are correlated with monetary policy and inflation in advanced industrial states, research by Cukierman, Webb, and Neyapti shows that such measures are not correlated in the developing countries.[2] Their findings suggest that legal rules may matter less than the incentives of those appointed to make monetary policy decisions. The independence of the Federal Reserve is not so much a function of its legal status as of its being closely connected to (indeed, owned by!) the financial sector. Contrast this institutional structure to the formal and informal ties that exist between the Russian central bank and both the Russian legislature and the state-owned enterprise sector.

A crucial question for regulatory policy, viewed politically, is not just what policy should be drafted, but what the regulatory structure and process that will draft and enforce those policies is going to look like. Who is enfranchised, and what consultative mechanisms exist? Without building some bases of consultation and support among affected sectors, it is unlikely that any reform effort will be consolidated.

REFERENCES

Cukierman, Alex, Steven B. Webb, and Belin Neyapti. 1992. "Measuring Central Bank Independence and Its Effect on Policy Outcomes." *World Bank Economic Review* 6(3): 353–98.

Haggard, Stephan, Chung Lee, and Sylvia Maxfield. 1993. *The Politics of Finance in Developing Countries.* Cornell University Press.

NOTES

1. Haggard, Lee, and Maxfield (1993).
2. Cukierman, Webb, and Neyapti (1992).

Chapter 6

LAWRENCE J. WHITE

Market Failures and Government Failures: Some Cautionary Implications for Financial Reform

There are almost as many concepts of sequencing in economic development as there are authors who address the topic. Virtually all discussions, however, involve recommendations for government actions—with respect to either intervention or deregulation and withdrawal. The financial sector is heavily regulated in virtually all countries—and especially so in developing countries. Much of the discussion of proper policy sequence thus involves financial reform issues directly (for example, should governments deregulate interest rates before or after other deregulatory actions) or indirectly (for example, should governments first deregulate international capital flows or trade flows?).[1] In this chapter I review the arguments concerning the appropriate sequence of financial sector reforms, taking care to place the discussion within the framework of government's role in economic development.[2] The second section sets the stage by sketching a stylized description of the process of economic growth and the role that the financial sector can play in that process. The third section reviews the arguments in favor of a competitive free market and then outlines the ways in which markets may fail to achieve the ideal outcome of the perfectly competitive markets. The fourth section categorizes the types of governmental intervention and links them to the topology of market failures and to applications in financial markets. I then discuss the types and sources of *government failure* and their applications to financial markets.[3] In the final section I distill the important lessons of this review and their applications.

The process of economic development (measured as growth in output per capita) is dependent on increases in physical and human

66

capital per capita, with the ability to absorb technological improvements production linked both to the level of human capital and to increases in physical capital. High private and public saving rates, with the savings converted into physical and human capital, are therefore critical factors in the growth process, as is the efficiency and productivity of the capital that is thereby created. An efficient financial sector will be an important element in generating savings and in converting savings into useful investments.[4]

The theoretical arguments supporting the microeconomists' ideal of a perfectly competitive market process are powerful. There is an "easy" case that can be made for government interventions to remedy the near-infinite market imperfections that can be found in any economy. But the analysis cannot stop there. Governments, too, are imperfect. As a result, the real-world policy choices are always between imperfect markets and imperfect governments, and economic theory alone cannot guide policy choices.

The case for government intervention is strongest where market imperfections are greatest, as in governmental provision of services such as police protection, national defense, children's education, roads, sewers, local public health services, and so on. The arguments for governmental provision of these services may be persuasive, but disagreements are likely to arise over other government interventions. For example, in such areas as tariffs, quotas, excise taxes, subsidies, licenses, price controls, limitations on entry, and mandates of various kinds designed to promote or curtail private sector activity are controversial, as is government ownership of facilities (for example, industrial plants or commercial banks) that could be privately owned. The principle that governments should be responsible for the safety-and-soundness (or prudential) regulation of banks and other depository institutions (and also for similar regulation of insurance companies and pension institutions) as well as be responsible for information regulation of securities markets receives widespread support, but restrictive and protectionist economic regulation of the financial sector provokes serious disagreement. Governmental interventions in various circumstances have improved market outcomes and fostered economic growth; in other cases, government interventions have seriously impeded growth.[5] In light of these latter experiences, skepticism about governmental intervention seems to have replaced the earlier belief in the virtues of an interventionist government as a central pillar in development strategy. The sequencing of government interventions seems afflicted with the same doubts.

FINANCIAL INSTITUTIONS AND THE DEVELOPMENT PROCESS

It is convenient to summarize the process of development by describing the economy's output as a function of its labor, the skills and knowledge embodied in that labor (that is, its human capital), its physical capital, its natural resources, any net foreign resources available to it, the technologies it uses, and the efficiency with which the inputs are combined. Growth in output arises from growth in inputs, advances in technologies (technological improvements that, in essence, allow more output to be produced from a given amount of inputs), and improvements in the efficiency with which existing resources and technologies are used.

The skills and knowledge embodied in an economy's labor force are related partly to levels of formal education (and the quality of that education) and partly to the skills and techniques learned on the job. As workers retire from the labor force, their human capital retires with them. In this way an economy's stock of human capital depreciates over time, and investments in the education and skill development of the entering labor force are required just to maintain a given stock of human capital in the economy. A growing labor force will require even larger investments to maintain the same average level of human capital per worker (frequently described as "capital widening"). Increases in the human capital levels per worker ("capital deepening") will require even greater investments.

The machinery, factories, and other productive facilities of an economy (for example, its rail lines, telecommunications lines, airports, harbors, roads, bridges, and tunnels) constitute its physical capital.[6] Over time physical capital depreciates from use and from natural causes (such as weather); consequently, continual investment is required to maintain a constant stock of physical capital. As is true of human capital, a growing labor force will require even higher levels of investment to maintain a constant level of physical capital per worker (capital widening). Similarly, increases in the amount of physical capital per worker (capital deepening) will require even higher levels of investment. To be a net recipient of foreign resources means that an economy is importing more goods and services than it is exporting. It can do so only if nonresidents are willing to provide donations or transfers to it or are prepared to invest in it.[7] In the latter case, the nonresidents obtain an equivalent claim on the economy's resources and will expect a profit or interest return on that claim. (They also retain the ability to dispose of that claim as they see fit, including the possibility of repatriating the resources.) Though an economy is likely to benefit from a net infusion of foreign investment, the net benefit is smaller than the nominal increase in output. Major technological advances are likely to be embodied in new equipment, necessitating investment in this equipment to reap the benefits of the new technology. Further, a better educated labor force is more likely to be adaptable and capable of absorbing technological changes, and some new technologies require highly skilled workers for their implementation.

The efficient and effective use of inputs to produce outputs is not automatic. Resources that are idle, underutilized, or misallocated imply a lower level of output than could otherwise be achieved. Similarly, investments in physical and human capital do not automatically yield higher outputs than would otherwise be possible. Ill-designed investments can mean a waste of resources and lower future levels of output than could otherwise be achieved. Examples would include factories that produce goods that cannot be sold at remunerative prices, buildings that cannot be sold or rented at remunerative levels, roads used by few vehicles, and labor skills that poorly fit the demands of an economy. Much of the debate concerning the role of government in the development process is focused on these efficiency questions: Is an economy that relies largely on markets to allocate its resources likely to achieve a more efficient transformation of its inputs into outputs, and a more efficient transformation of its savings into efficient investments for future outputs? Or are major government interventions necessary, or at least more likely to achieve more efficient outcomes? This is my focus in the next two sections of this chapter.

My discussion has been in terms of aggregate output and the growth of aggregate output of an economy. For the purposes of economic development, output per capita and output per worker (and their rates of growth) are more relevant. For these measures, aggregate output must be scaled to a country's population or to its labor force; growth or labor force growth rates will affect the scaled-output growth rate measures. To the extent that an economy can generate a high rate of saving and can channel that saving to domestic investment (in both physical and human capital), this will follow, because of the direct effect of the additions to physical and human capital and the indirect effect of the capital additions in facilitating technological change. The more efficient the transformation of the saving into productive investment, the higher the growth of output for any given rate of saving; indeed, the growth rate may well be the primary indication of the transformation's efficiency. But even inefficiencies in the transformation of inputs into outputs can be overcome by higher rates of saving. In essence, a high rate of saving can cover a multitude of efficiency errors in an economy. Conversely, widespread efficiency errors can undermine the effects of an otherwise respectable saving rate.

The efficiency of the financial sector will be a central factor in economic growth. Finance is ubiquitous. Enterprises, large or small, must obtain some form of financing for their capital stock—plant, equipment, machinery, factories, inventories, and so on. Small and start-up enterprises are likely to have to rely on informal sources of finance. Larger and more seasoned enterprises are more likely to be able to count on formal institutions, especially banks. The largest enterprises may be able to tap securities markets. The degree of the information "opaqueness" of the borrowers—ranging from most opaque for the small and start-up enterprises to least opaque for the largest and most seasoned enterprises—is an important determinant of their abilities to obtain finance from the various potential sources. Throughout this process, financial institutions and financial facilitators will gather and allocate society's savings. If this allocation is done efficiently, productive enterprises will receive financing and will grow and prosper. The efficient financial sector thus enhances the quality of an economy's savings and investment, thereby encouraging economic growth. Conversely, an inefficient financial sector channels savings in inefficient directions and thereby acts as a drag on growth.[8]

MARKET EFFICIENCIES AND
MARKET FAILURES

In an economy of gain-seeking individuals, the argument for relying on markets to provide the signals and incentives for resource allocation decisions is a powerful one. However, it has its limitations. The argument for reliance on market outcomes rests on a number of assumptions: Individuals are gain-seeking and know their own best interests; individuals are the full beneficiaries of their own actions and bear the full costs; they can easily enter into enforceable contracts, including the ability to organize themselves into production units (firms) that combine labor, capital, expertise, and other resources to produce and sell outputs of goods and services; and there are a large number of buyers and sellers of all goods and services, and entry into the market is easy. The interactions of demand and supply in markets will theoretically yield prices that provide the incentives and signals for efficient production and consumption decisions.[9] Consumers will arrange their consumption of goods and services so that the marginal unit of income yields the same amount of satisfaction among all choices. The equilibrium market prices and quantities thus yield an outcome where the economy's marginal costs of production (representing its opportunity costs—the value of the forgone opportunities to produce other goods and services) are just equal to consumers' marginal willingness to pay (representing their marginal satisfaction). No rearrangement of production within or among markets can improve upon this outcome; no alternative set of outputs can yield a greater level of aggregate satisfaction among those individuals in the economy.[10]

The process and the outcome just described pertain to the allocation of resources in output markets at a particular time. But similar arguments would apply to input markets and to the allocation of resources across time periods. In the latter case, gain-seeking individuals will make saving and investment decisions across time in light of the opportunities open to them and the interest rates in the market.

But actual markets can fail to achieve the promised efficient outcome, because one or more of the assumptions might not be satisfied. If only one or a few producers are present in the market and entry is not easy, the market outcome is likely to involve a lower production level and a higher price than the perfectly competitive outcome.[11] The market price will now exceed the marginal cost of production, and the level of production will therefore be too small and thus inefficient.[12] Though economies of scale can be a source of market power, they can also be a source of inefficiency even if a seller does not set prices so as to exploit its market power.[13] Moreover, market outcomes can involve too much production or consumption activity as a result of uncompensated costs imposed on others. Air and water pollutant emissions by producers, air pollutant emissions by motorists, and the traffic congestion produced by motorists' use of roads at peak periods are familiar examples of negative externalities. The mirror image—positive externalities—implies too little production or consumption; public goods involve pervasive positive externalities. Inadequate knowledge or its asymmetric distribution among market participants can also lead to distortions in market outcomes. Virtually all actual markets are likely to embody some failings and will therefore not achieve the completely efficient outcomes of the ideal market.

This listing of potential market failures can be readily applied to the financial sector, especially in developing countries. Indeed, in these economies market failure in the financial sector is pervasive. There are often few formal financial institutions, and they may each exercise significant market power. Economies of scale for financial institutions are important in the smaller economies of many developing countries. Dealing with the negative externalities of depositor runs and of investor misinformation is critical for the financial sector. Uncertainty and information asymmetry are pervasive in developing countries. The factors that help financial institutions pierce this information fog in developed economies—standardized accounting systems and well-developed commercial legal frameworks—are likely to be only rudimentary in most developing countries. The less educated populations of developing countries may be unable to make complex financial decisions that are in their own best long-run interest or to find reliable agents to assist them.

The potential for government action in the financial sector to remedy these market imperfections thus appears substantial at first glance. Indeed, the financial sector has been an area of extensive government intervention in virtually all economies, developed and developing alike. But, as we shall see, the real-world limitations on governments' abilities often have created outcomes that have worsened rather than improved upon market outcomes. Indeed, some of the market imperfections in the financial sector, such as monopoly-oligopoly, can often be traced to government actions (for example, artificial barriers to market entry).

GOVERNMENT INTERVENTION AND GOVERNMENT FAILURES

In principle, governmental intervention corrects for the various failings of markets. But governmental intervention can also make outcomes worse. Government can directly provide a good or service as a substitute for private production. This form of intervention would be best suited to dealing with the problems of monopoly, economies of scale, or public goods; but government provision could seek to remedy any of the market failures discussed here. To the extent that a government does not or cannot charge prices for its output that cover the full costs, however, that government will have to levy taxes elsewhere that will discourage output in those other areas and be a source of inefficiency. Alternatively, the government may fund shortfalls through borrowing, thereby absorbing savings that otherwise could have been devoted to productive investments; again, this opportunity cost must be included in any calculation of net benefits. The funding for government programs might also come through inflationary finance ("printing money"), thereby levying an implicit tax on the rest of the economy and creating the inefficiencies associated with inflationary macroeconomies.

Because an excise tax adds to the cost of producing a good or service, the tax is a way of discouraging the activity. It is best suited to dealing with the problems of negative externalities and serving a regulatory function.[14] Conversely, by reducing the cost of production or consumption, subsidies encourage an activity. They are thus best suited for dealing with the problems of economies of scale, positive externalities, or stimulating the production of any deemed public goods.[15] A government would have to raise the funds for the subsidy through taxation (or borrowing) elsewhere in the economy, however, so the distortion created by that taxation must again be taken into account.

Regulation, by limiting or mandating some activities directly, can influence production or consumption. Economic regulation usually entails government controls over prices, profits, and entry.[16] It is best designed to deal with market failure resulting from market power. Familiar examples involve the price and profit regulation of local electricity, natural gas, water, and telephone services. But economic regulation often extends far beyond the boundaries of monopoly regulation. A second category, health-safety-environment regulation, usually involves direct administrative controls over production processes and product or service types.[17] Familiar examples include environmental regulations, air and water pollutant emissions, workplace safety, controls on food additives and pharmaceutical distribution, and safety-and-soundness (prudential) regulation of banks and other financial institutions. A third category is information regulation; food package labeling and corporate securities disclosure requirements are familiar examples.

All of the various forms of government intervention listed here can be found in the financial sectors of most developing economies. Government ownership of some—sometimes most or even all—formal financial institutions (such as banks and other depositories, insurance companies, and pension institutions) is common. Government taxation of some types of financial transactions may discourage them or be outright prohibitive. Explicit subsidies (rather than the implicit subsidies that arise from differential taxation or regulation) are rare, probably because government revenues are usually scarce. But regulation is pervasive. The ubiquity of financial regulation warrants further analysis.

Economic regulation includes government controls over "prices"—interest rates on loans or deposits, fees on loan transactions or insurance transactions, and so on; limits on entry (such as limits on who can establish a de novo financial institution); limits on location; limits on the types of activities that can be undertaken by financial institutions; and limits on foreigners' entry, scale, or scope with respect to financial institution operations. It also includes the "must serve" requirements (for example, with respect to types of customers or their geographic locations) often imposed on banks and other financial institutions in both developing and developed countries. Safety-and-soundness regulation includes the provision of minimum net worth (capital) requirements on banks and insurance companies and limitations on activities and investments deemed especially risky.

There are also information requirements that issuers of traded securities should reveal specified types of information about themselves and their activities at the time of the issuance of the securities and at periodic intervals (for example, quarterly or annually) thereafter. This also encompasses requirements that banks provide their loan and deposit customers with standardized statements of interest rates; that mutual fund (unit trust) operators provide customers with standardized statements as to yield and recent performance; that life insurance companies provide prospective policyholders with standardized fee and yield information; and so on.

Though government intervention can in principle improve the efficiency outcomes of imperfect markets, governments too can fail to deliver their promised outcomes, and their efforts at intervention can cause an economy's efficiency to deteriorate rather than increase. Without the specific profit goal that motivates most private enterprises, government agencies—buffeted by diffuse and conflicting goals—all too often issue conflicting mandates that are difficult to understand or implement. Again, without the specific profit goal, the diffuse goals of government agencies often create disincentives to effective action. Societal values concerning income distribution and equality of incomes are likely to hold sway in the public sector, making a link between wages and performance difficult to achieve in government behavior. To be effective, organizations have to be managed effectively. With diffuse goals, government agencies are difficult to manage. In any event, effective management is a relatively scarce skill that usually commands premium wages in an economy.[18] The egalitarian ethos that makes performance-linked pay difficult to implement in government agencies also means that those in low-skill jobs are usually overpaid compared with their private market counterparts, and those in high-skill jobs are underpaid. As a consequence, governments frequently have difficulties in attracting and retaining highly skilled individuals, including managers, and government effectiveness suffers as a consequence.[19]

Government agencies are clearly no better at acquiring and using information than are private sector entities.[20] Indeed, the problems of incentives and of management I have described suggest that government agencies may well have substantial difficulties in using information. With inadequate information, government provision of goods and services will mean inappropriate quantities, qualities, and prices. Similarly, government taxes and subsidies may undershoot or overshoot their targets; substantial overshooting could cause inefficiency to ripple through the economy. Regulatory controls based on poor information are especially troublesome.[21]

In an economy of gain-seeking individuals, those who are significantly affected by government action are unlikely to remain passive. Instead, they are likely to try to influence the processes of government to achieve outcomes favorable to themselves. They will find it worthwhile to expend considerable resources (ranging from outright bribery and corruption to more subtle lobbying and promises of electoral support) to twist government actions in their favor. Rent-seeking behavior is particularly common in transitional societies, where the rules of the game are unclear and susceptible to insider manipulation.[22] The wider the area of economic activity in which governmental intervention is deemed legitimate and accepted, the greater the potential for these rent-seeking efforts. Comparatively small groups of individuals who are intensely affected by government actions will have the most to gain from organizing themselves to influence government policy.[23] Their success in achieving regulatory protection, import protection, or subsidies will be at the expense of the general public.

The general problems of government failure apply with particular force to government interventions into the financial sector. Economic regulation, which is applied extensively to the financial sector worldwide, rarely addresses true monopoly or market power problems. Instead, the common interest rate controls, protective limitations on entry, and must-serve and other requirements have been almost always motivated by income distribution goals created by pressure from interest groups. This has been true in developed countries as well as in developing countries. Government ownership and operation of financial institutions, which is common in developing countries, routinely brings with it the pressures for income distribution. These forms of intervention into financial markets have almost always brought substantial *decreases* rather than improvements in the efficiency of the affected financial markets.[24] For seven developing Asian countries, the deleterious consequences of extensive economic regulation on their financial markets during the 1970s and 1980s has recently been documented by the Asian Development Bank.[25]

With respect to safety-and-soundness regulation of financial institutions, the limitations of government information, knowledge, staffing, and management have had adverse consequences for the efficiency of financial markets, especially when interest group pressures are involved. Concern for crucial safety-and-soundness issues—such as the role of economic incentives, adequate levels of net worth (capital), and adequate regulatory oversight of risky lending and investment decisions—may be neglected at the same time, with the result that widespread insolvencies of banks and other depository institutions and of insurance companies are common.[26] Insolvencies are a glaring indication of the inefficiency of the original investment decisions. Again, the experiences of seven Asian countries—six of which have had serious problems of explicit or implicit financial institution insolvencies—has been documented.[27]

Finally, the neglect of information regulation by the governments of many developing countries—that is, failing to pay attention to the role of accounting and of disclosure generally—has meant that their securities markets have languished. This neglect is understandable; the skills to administer an effective information regulatory framework are scarce in most developing countries. During the 1970s and 1980s, the neglect of securities markets was consistent with the goals of interventionist-minded governments, which saw banks as their primary vehicle for channeling their economies' flows of saving and investment. The governments saw securities markets as unruly and less susceptible to direct control. As a result, they were content to see securities markets languish in the absence of effective information regulation and be perceived as risky by the public.[28] In sum, government failures have been pervasive with respect to the financial sector in many countries, and especially so in the developing countries.

THE LESSONS AND THEIR APPLICATIONS

Clearly, imperfect markets have their counterpart in imperfect governments. There is no automatic assurance that government intervention will improve on the outcomes of imperfect markets. There is a presumption that government intervention can improve matters when market failures are more serious. In certain public goods areas (for example, national defense, local police protection, public health, and roads and sewerage) and in areas where substantial positive externalities (such as in education and in basic research in fields important to an economy) or substantial negative externalities prevail (such as with significant air and water pollution problems), some government provision or intervention generally seems warranted. The provision of a stable macroeconomic environment and a system of enforceable property rights are indisputably important functions of government.

But even in the areas of prescriptive public goods, government intervention can take on many questionable shapes and forms and go in many directions. In the areas where the failings of markets are less severe, the presumption in favor of government intervention inevitably weakens. A few examples should clarify these points. On first impression, it would appear that the provision of roads is an important governmental function; indeed, governments universally provide public thoroughfares. But substantial resources can be wasted through poor design, faulty construction, or inadequate maintenance. Superhighways that lead nowhere and that are hardly used are a poor use of an economy's scarce resources. Faulty construction with inappropriate materials, or inadequate maintenance, can mean that excessive resources will be required for reconstruction or upkeep or that the road cannot be used to its full effectiveness. Under some circumstances a private toll road might be an alternative to one that is built and maintained by the government. The electronics (and economics) of the metering of motor vehicles' usage of roads are becoming increasingly feasible, making the pricing of road usage—and, ultimately, the private construction and operation of roads—worthy of serious consideration.

Further, incentive issues are important when considering public and private alternatives in information creation, collection, and dissemination. Private entities will have the direct incentives to seek out the information that they find most worthwhile. The incentives for public sector employees to seek out information are more problematic. To bolster private sector information creation, governments could adopt and enforce a legal framework that recognizes and supports intellectual property (for example, patents, copyrights, and trademarks).

Industries characterized by only a handful of firms (oligopolies) and by barriers to entry will likely behave in ways that are less efficient than the model of perfect competition promises.[29] Can government intervention—for example, economic regulation—realistically improve matters? The experience of the United States in regulating a number of such industries and then deregulating them in the 1970s and early 1980s suggests that government failure had been substantial and that the unregulated markets have been significantly more efficient than their regulated predecessors.[30] Statements about the necessity for government intervention should be greeted with caution.[31] Empirical evidence and practical experience are the appropriate guides to policy choice.

Finally, with respect to sequencing, a clear inference from my argument is that economic development policies generally should not rely heavily on sequenced governmental interventions. The potential pitfalls of government failure are likely to be too great. One cannot expect fine-tuning measures to work precisely as intended. Indeed, the opposite course—a lessening of government intervention (such as reductions in economic regulation, expanded privatization, and reduced taxes and subsidies)—would be more appropriate. And even with the reductions in government intervention, reliance on finely tuned sequencing of deregulation actions is probably ill advised. Instead, an orderly withdrawal—but with all deliberate speed—is likely to be preferable.[32] The Asian Development Bank study indicates that the sequencing of the economic deregulation of the financial sector in the seven Asian nations studied has been much less important than their commitment to and speedy execution of deregulation and privatization.[33]

One important exception to these admonitions should be noted: As economic deregulation of financial institutions (especially banks and insurance companies) proceeds, *heightened* safety-and-soundness regulation is necessary. Economic deregulation can give the owners and managers of financial institutions the opportunities to pursue more efficient, less risky strategies. But the new opportunities can also be used to pursue more risky strategies (and lower net worth levels make this latter pursuit increasingly likely). Heightened safety-and-soundness regulation is therefore necessary and should proceed concurrently; ideally, it should even be in place as the general deregulation occurs.[34] In sum, markets and the incentives they create are powerful forces for allocating resources in an economy composed of gain-seeking individuals. Though there is always an important role for government, the forces of government failure are at least as powerful as those of market failure. Government actions in economic development, including in particular any finely tuned sequencing actions, should proceed cautiously indeed.

REFERENCES

Amsden, Alice. 1989. *Asia's Next Giant: South Korea and Late Industrialization.* Oxford University Press.

Asian Development Bank. 1995. *Asian Development Outlook 1995.* Oxford University Press.

Bardhan, Pranab. 1990. "Symposium on the State and Economic Development." *Journal of Economic Perspectives* 4 (Summer): 3–7.

Baron, David P. 1989. "Design of Regulatory Mechanisms and Institutions." In *Handbook of Industrial Organization,* vol. 2, edited by Richard Schmalensee and Robert D. Willig, ch. 24. Amsterdam: North Holland.

Braeutigam, Ronald R. 1989. "Optimal Policies for Natural Monopolies." In *Handbook of Industrial Organization,* vol. 2, edited by Richard Schmalensee and Robert D. Willig, ch. 23. Amsterdam: North Holland.

Datta-Chaudhuri, Mrinal. 1990. "Market Failure and Government Failure." *Journal of Economic Perspectives* 4 (Summer): 25–39.

Fishlow, Albert, 1990. "The Latin American State." *Journal of Economic Perspectives* 4 (Summer): 61–74.

Fry, Maxwell J. 1988. *Money, Interest, and Banking in Economic Development.* Johns Hopkins University Press.

_____ . 1989. "Financial Development: Theories and Recent Experience." *Oxford Review of Economic Policy* 5 (Winter): 29–54.

Fudenberg, Drew, and Jean Tirole. 1989. "Noncooperative Game Theory for Industrial Organization: An Introduction and Overview." In *Handbook of Industrial Organization,* vol. 1, edited by Richard Schmalensee and Robert D. Willig, ch. 5. Amsterdam: North Holland.

Gruenspecht, Howard K., and Lester B. Lave. 1989. "The Economics of Health, Safety, and Environmental Regulation." In *Handbook of Industrial Organiza-*

tion, vol. 2, edited by Richard Schmalensee and Robert D. Willig, ch. 26. Amsterdam: North Holland.

Jacquemin, Alexis, and Margaret E. Slade. 1989. "Cartels, Collusion, and Horizontal Merger." In *Handbook of Industrial Organization,* vol. 1, edited by Richard Schmalensee and Robert D. Willig, ch. 7. Amsterdam: North Holland.

Japan Overseas Economic Cooperation Fund. 1992–93. "Issues Related to the World Bank's Approach to Structural Adjustment—Proposal from a Major Partner." *OECF Research Quarterly* 73.

Joskow, Paul L., and Nancy L. Rose. 1989. "The Effects of Economic Regulation." In *Handbook of Industrial Organization,* vol. 2, edited by Richard Schmalensee and Robert D. Willig, ch. 25. Amsterdam: North Holland.

Joskow, Paul L., and Roger G. Noll. 1994. "Economic Regulation: Deregulation and Regulatory Reform During the 1980s." In *American Economic Policy in the 1980s,* edited by Martin Feldstein, 367–440. University of Chicago Press.

Krueger, Anne O. 1974. "The Political Economy of the Rent-Seeking Society." *American Economic Review* 66 (June): 291–303.

_____ . 1990. "Government Failures in Development." *Journal of Economic Perspectives* 4 (Summer): 9–23.

Kuznets, Paul W. 1988. "An East Asian Model of Economic Development: Japan, Taiwan, and South Korea." *Economic Development and Cultural Change* 36 (supplement): 511–43.

McKinnon, Ronald I. 1991. *The Order of Economic Liberalization: Financial Control in the Transition to a Market Economy.* Johns Hopkins University Press.

Noll, Roger G. 1989. "Economic Perspectives on the Politics of Regulation." In *Handbook of Industrial Organization,* vol. 2, edited by Richard Schmalense and Robert D. Willig, ch. 22. Amsterdam: North Holland.

Pack, Howard, and Larry E. Westphal. 1986. "Industrial Strategy and Technological Change: Theory Versus Reality." *Journal of Development Economics* 22 (June): 87–128.

Peltzman, Sam. 1976. "Toward a More General Theory of Regulation." *Journal of Law and Economics* 19 (August): 211–40.

Posner, Richard A. 1974. "Theories of Economic Regulation." *Bell Journal of Economics and Management Science* 5 (Autumn): 335–58.

Schmalensee, Richard, and Robert D. Willig. 1989. *Handbook of Industrial Organization,* vols. 1 and 2. Amsterdam: North Holland.

Sen, Amartya. 1990. "Development Strategies: The Roles of the State and the Private Sector." *Proceedings of the World Bank Annual Conference on Development Economics.*

Shapiro, Carl. 1989. "Theories of Oligopoly Behavior." In *Handbook of Industrial Organization*, vol. 1, edited by Richard Schmalensee and Robert D. Willig, ch. 6. Amsterdam: North Holland.

Smith, Stephen C. 1991. "Industrial Policy in Developing Countries: Reconsidering the Real Sources of Export-Led Growth." Cambridge, Mass.: Economic Policy Institute.

Stern, Nicholas. 1990. "Development Strategies: The Roles of the State and the Private Sector." *Proceedings of the World Bank Annual Conference on Development Economics.*

Stigler, George J. 1971. "The Theory of Regulation." *Bell Journal of Economics and Management Science* 2 (1971): 3–21.

Stiglitz, Joseph E. 1988. "Economic Organization, Information, and Development." In *Handbook of Development Economics*, vol. 1, edited by Hollis Chanery and T. N. Srinivasan, ch. 5. Amsterdam: North Holland.

_____. 1990. "Development Strategies: The Roles of the State and the Private Sector." *Proceedings of the World Bank Annual Conference on Development Economics*, 430–33.

Wade, Robert. 1990. *Governing the Market: Economic Theory and the Role of Government in East Asian Industrialization.* Princeton University Press.

Westphal, Larry E. 1990. "Industrial Policy in an Export-Propelled Economy: Lessons from South Korea's Experience." *Journal of Economic Perspectives* 4 (Summer): 41–59.

White, Lawrence J. 1986. "The Partial Deregulation of Banks and Other Depository Institutions." In *Regulatory Reform: What Actually Happened*, edited by Leonard W. Weiss and Michael W. Klass, 169–204. Boston: Little, Brown.

_____. 1991. *The S&L Debacle: Public Policy Lessons for Bank and Thrift Regulation.* Oxford University Press.

_____. 1993. "A Cautionary Tale of Deregulation Gone Awry: The S&L Debacle." *Southern Economic Journal* 59 (January): 496–514.

_____. 1994. "U.S. Banking Regulation: Multiple Dimensions, Multiple Consequences." In *International Financial Market Regulation*, edited by Benn Steil. Wiley.

_____. 1995. "The Financial Sector in Developing Countries in Asia." In *Financial Sector Development in Asia*, edited by Shahid Zahid. Oxford University Press.

_____. Forthcoming. "Government-Business Relationships in the U.S. in the 1980s." In *U.S.-Japan Economic Forum*, vol. 2, edited by Martin Feldstein and Ytaka Kosai. University of Chicago Press.

Winston, Clifford. 1993. "Economic Deregulation: Days of Reckoning for Microeconomists." *Journal of Economic Literature* 31 (September): 1263–89.

Wolf, C., Jr. 1989. *Markets or Governments: Choosing between Imperfect Alternatives.* MIT Press.

World Bank Operations Evaluation Department. 1992. "World Bank Support for Industrialization in Korea, India, and Indonesia."

Zahid, Shahid. 1995. *Financial Sector Development in Asia.* Oxford University Press.

NOTES

1. For symposia, see Bardhan (1990); Krueger (1990); Datta-Chaudhuri (1990); Westphal (1990); Fishlow (1990); Sen (1990); Stern (1990); Stiglitz (1990).

2. See, for example, McKinnon (1991).

3. For a somewhat similar discussion of market failure and government failure, see Wolf (1989).

4. A more efficient financial sector means greater economic growth potential from existing savings or equal growth potential from reduced savings. See, for example, White (1995); Asian Development Bank (1995).

5. For the pro-intervention arguments, see, for example, Amsden (1989); Wade (1990); Smith (1991); World Bank Operations Evaluation Department (1992); Japan Overseas Economic Cooperation Fund (1992). For "revisionist" analyses that reach different conclusion, see Pack and Westphal (1986); Kuznets (1988); Westphal (1990).

6. In addition, stocks of inventories are usually counted as capital, because they are essential for smoothing production flows. Increases in inventories are counted as investment.

7. These transfers would include the remittances by overseas nationals to their domestic relatives.

8. See, for example, White (1995); Asian Development Bank (1995).

9. Resources that cannot be easily expanded and that are scarce in relation to the economy's demands on them—for example, productive land, mineral deposits, special skills—will earn rents that reflect that scarcity.

10. This statement makes the strong assumption that aggregate satisfaction is the simple sum of the satisfactions of the individuals in the economy and that the latter are all measurable in terms of their willingness to pay for and supply goods and services to the economy.

11. For overviews, see Schmalensee and Willig (1989).

12. If, however, a country has market power in a product or service vis-à-vis its international trading partners, that market power can be exploited by the

country to its benefit (provided that its trading partners do not retaliate). In this instance the country would want to restrict the foreign sales of the good or service below the levels that a competitive industry would otherwise provide.

13. Similar problems arise if there is monopsony or oligopsony in a market: one or a few buyers.

14. For example, an export excise tax would be a way of reducing output to exploit the monopoly gains vis-à-vis trading partners mentioned in note 12.

15. In principle, a subsidy could be a solution to the inefficiency problem of monopoly. In practice, the income distribution consequences would likely be considered to be unacceptable.

16. For overviews, see Braeutigam (1989); Joskow and Rose (1989).

17. For an overview, see Gruenspecht and Lave (1989).

18. Further, if a shortage of entrepreneurial and managerial skills is considered to be a problem for private sector activity in an economy, nationalizing the activity or placing it under heavy regulation does not eliminate the shortage but only changes its immediate locus.

19. Government agencies may be able to attract some highly skilled individuals who hope to acquire the specific skills related to government operation and then leave to use those skills in the private sector. For example, the U.S. government has been able to attract young lawyers, even though its entry-level pay scale has been below the levels of the private sector alternatives for these lawyers. But the flow of skilled human resources at senior levels is usually one-way—from government to the private sector—with the exception of short-term political appointments. The exceptions to this overall pattern are individuals who strongly believe that government service has an important intrinsic value and are willing to enter and remain in government service despite unfavorable pay differentials vis-à-vis the private sector.

20. For overviews and further discussion, see Stiglitz (1988; 1990).

21. For an overview, see Baron (1989).

22. See Krueger (1974). For an overview, see Noll (1989).

23. See Stigler (1971); Posner (1974); Peltzman (1976). For an overview, see Noll (1989).

24. For the U.S. experience, see White (1986; 1994).

25. See Zahid (1995); Asian Development Bank (1995). The seven countries are India, Indonesia, Korea, Pakistan, the Philippines, Taiwan, and Thailand. For other discussions and examples, see Fry (1988; 1989); McKinnon (1991).

26. For the U.S. experience, see White (1991; 1993). The United States is not alone among developed countries in having to deal with bank insolvencies. In the early 1990s the governments of Japan, France, Sweden, Finland, and Spain have all had to cover the insolvency losses of major banks in their countries.

27. See Zahid (1995); Asian Development Bank (1995). The one country among the seven that did not experience serious insolvency problems was Taiwan. Also, Venezuela and Mexico have had to deal with financial institution insolvencies in the 1990s, and Chile experienced major problems a decade earlier.

28. See Zahid (1995); Asian Development Bank (1995).

29. For overviews, see Fudenberg and Tirole (1989); Shapiro (1989); Jacquemin and Slade (1989).

30. For overviews, see Joskow and Rose (1989); Winston (1993); Joskow and Noll (1994); White (forthcoming).

31. Alas, at least one influential report has not heeded this admonition; see Japan Overseas Economic Cooperation Fund (1992).

32. The promises of success that accompany withdrawal ought not to be overly broad or effusive. In the aftermath of the deregulation of an industry, for example, there are likely to be some losers (firms that fail, buyers or suppliers that are disadvantaged, and the like) as well as winners. This is a near-inevitable part of a transition from a less efficient industry with misallocated resources, and with firms that were adapted to the regulatory regime and are ill adapted to a deregulated environment, to a more efficient industry. See Joskow and Rose (1989); White (1993); Joskow and Noll (1994).

33. See Zahid (1995); Asian Development Bank (1995).

34. See White (1991; 1993).

Chapter 7

PHILIP A. WELLONS

Sequencing Legal Development to Support Financial Sector Reforms

The sequencing of law reform to support financial sector development is an important subject largely ignored in the literature.[1] Law reform and finance are the major work of Harvard Law School's Program on International Financial Systems. We have completed comparative studies about the way government policy shaped the development of money and capital markets in East and Southeast Asia over the last three decades and have been advising governments of transitional countries about commercial and financial law development, including Bulgaria, Laos, and Kazakhstan. We have examined the need of eastern European countries for training and technical assistance in law.

This experience, as well as other experiments in law development, made us reluctant to generalize. Nevertheless, I will now do just that, discussing how things might be and how they are today in transitional countries, notably in eastern Europe and the new independent states of the former Soviet Union.

In an ideal world, a country's financial policymakers design a financial development strategy. Lawyers then weed out archaic laws and prepare appropriate financial laws as well as the necessary infrastructure, phasing in both to support the financial development strategy.

The reality is disorderly and ad hoc. A typical scenario would have someone from a regional stock exchange in France visit the country's finance minister. He offers to sell the exchange's stock trading system, funded with a subsidized French export credit and a grant. He offers, at no extra cost, a securities law and stock exchange law; his group had just written them for Poland. The finance minister has no one on his staff who understands capital market policy. The World Bank finan-

86

cial mission has not finished its report yet. The privatization program is starting up. This is a quick solution to many problems. The minister accepts, and as a result the country has new financial laws not tailored to the country's needs. The sequence of law development does not always follow this path, but it also does not fit the ideal pattern. But what should that ideal be?

ELEMENTS OF LAW DEVELOPMENT THAT NEED A SEQUENCE

Sequencing issues arise for both the content of the law and the legal process.[2] Many discussions of financial law development in transitional economies are devoted largely to the need for specific laws: a banking law or a securities law. This is too narrow.

The content of the law refers both to laws governing the financial sector and laws governing other commercial activities. Examples of financial laws are those for banks, securities markets, and institutional investors. Other commercial laws are extensive, from bankruptcy to trusts law. A simple list of titles would cover more than a page.

The legal process includes legislative drafting, implementation, and enforcement. Drafting laws is just that. Implementation is the work by government agencies or their surrogates—self-regulatory organizations (SROs)—so the law works as designed. A company law may need a companies registry, for example, and a banking law needs prudential rules and examiners. Stock exchanges need internal rules for brokers. Enforcement is often through courts, initiated by private or public entities. But it may also take the form of binding arbitration, recognized by the courts, or nonbinding mediation. The issues of legal process are nontrivial because process creates the law as applied rather than merely as written. It is the applied law that influences behavior.

There is a third type of sequencing issues that I do not discuss in detail here. Economic law requires the commitment of many people to its precepts, so people must know of it. Many transitional governments still do not even publish all their decrees. The law developer must decide the sequence for reaching the audiences. One such sequence would be first the government officials who draft or implement, followed by enforcers, private lawyers and people in business, savers and users of funds, and the public at large. This is an important type of sequencing that gets little attention.

CONTENT: SEQUENCING FINANCIAL AND COMMERCIAL LAWS

Law development theory offers little guidance about the sequencing of substantive laws for financial reform. Competing theories yield a few guidelines at a broad level of generalization about the relation of law to economic development. From these one might extrapolate to the financial sector. One view is that law evolves with the economy; as economies converge, so does law.[3] This notion suggests a sequence in that converging financial systems would require similar laws. If one knows the laws of the prototype financial system, one could perhaps identify an order for supplying laws a country needs. Unfortunately, this view offers little operational guidance. A competing view is that laws are a function of many idiosyncratic currents in any country's development and are therefore unique to each country.[4] In this view, one cannot extrapolate from a reform sequence that worked for one country to an appropriate sequence for another country, particularly if the traditions of the two differ fundamentally.

Turning to current practice, one sees two tendencies today in the sequence of law and financial development in transition countries. First, people concerned with financial reform tend to emphasize financial laws over other commercial laws, so the latter receive attention after the former. Work on banking laws started early and moved faster in many countries; commercial law efforts followed later. This was natural when the advisers' mandate was financial sector reform. It was also strategic: domestic financial resources had to be gathered quickly.

Second, people reforming law tend not to coordinate the development of financial law with that of commercial law. The result is that sequencing is haphazard. There are several reasons for this poor coordination, some prosaic. Different ministries are responsible for different laws, the finance ministry and central bank often taking the lead on financial laws and the justice ministry or cabinet of ministers on commercial law. Different donors fund financial and commercial reform. Sometimes it seems that one donor says, "You work with the central bank and I'll work with the justice ministry," and that is the last conversation they have. Having different advisers on a project often hinders coordination. Specialists in financial law and those in commercial law are rarely able to advise on one another's topics. Rivalry among the players creates serious complications. The French and the Germans seem to think that their legal experts, rather than those from the United States, should lead in eastern Europe. Multilateral donors sometimes see each other as competitors and do not cooperate. Different private subcontractors on one project can be the worst offenders; the rivalry among advisers can exacerbate host country divisions. When the ministers of finance and justice both want to be prime minister, cooperation is rare.

The lack of coordination may be one of the greatest impediments to a reasonable sequence for law development. This chaos cannot be called strength in diversity. A better alternative to chaos or financial-laws-first is for a government or aid donor to focus on a specific set of financial activities and develop the related commercial laws. The focus will vary with the country's needs, but a simple illustration is the choice between developing direct or indirect finance.

Assume that indirect finance, through intermediaries, should be promoted. One donor, for example, decided to focus its business law development projects on credit. This means the donor worked on banking laws (among financial laws) and on laws for secured transactions and bankruptcy (among other commercial laws). The rationale is that credit requires the ability to take security and to foreclose on delinquent debtors. One might add mortgage law and (necessarily) land law to the list, plus a checking law. We assume that a law governs the central bank, contracts can be made, corporate liability is limited, and property rights are respected—that is, basic laws are also in place. The list could be extended, but these laws are the essentials.

An emphasis on direct finance would promote the money and capital markets instead of the intermediated markets. This would lead to work on financial laws governing securities, stock exchanges, and institutional investors (pension funds, insurance companies, and mutual funds). Among commercial laws, one needs a negotiable instruments law so that rights in securities could be transferred predictably, the basic constitutional protection of property rights, the company law to establish shareholder rights and obligations, contracts law, and laws governing fiduciaries like brokers. Other laws would be helpful but seem less critical. A bankruptcy law would be useful, though the market could value the securities even in its absence.

In short, a strategy to develop direct finance results in a different constellation of laws—even commercial laws—than a strategy for indirect finance, although both require the same basic laws. The sequence of law development varies depending on the financial strategy.

The choice between indirect and direct financial systems may seem abstract, but models for each are pushed today. The most prominent examples of indirect financial systems, Japan and Germany, appeal to many developing countries. The United States offers a contrary model, a system with vibrant direct financing through money and capital markets. Both models compete within individual transition countries now, which complicates the sequence of law development.

We could go a step further and search, within any individual law, for a sequence to adopt elements that would be useful in transition countries. For example, could a country first write a securities law that dealt only with issuance and trading of simple securities, then later amend or supplement the law for more esoteric matters, such as rules governing takeovers? The advantage is that stripped-down laws are more easily managed by executive and legislative branches with tiny staffs of limited experience. The law could take effect faster than a more complex one. Arguing against this approach is that abuses start early and subsequent legislation may be inordinately delayed. Experienced legislative drafting advisers do simplify the laws to fit the country's needs and capabilities. I doubt that we can find ways to divide a law in advance into must-have-early and wait-until-later parts that would speed drafting much. One writes a simple law but includes all basic items.

SEQUENCING DEVELOPMENT
OF THE LEGAL PROCESS

Sequencing issues for the legal process have had a different pattern. For commercial and financial law, the tendency has been to concentrate first on legislative drafting, then move to implementation and later to enforcement. My sense is that overall the resources funded drafting first and most of all, with some funding of implementation and very little for enforcement. The logic for this sequence seems impeccable; how can you implement or enforce a law that does not exist? It is indeed a waste of time to prepare implementing regulations for a draft law that, once passed, differs greatly from the draft used. The problem with this sequence is also simple: What is the use of a law that, once passed, cannot be implemented or enforced? Transitional governments lack a general capacity to implement law or a judiciary ready for a new securities law. The governments often have limited or no staff to carry out the legislative mandate. The courts lack the capacity to decide these issues: the judges are ignorant of markets and the basic concepts of the new law and are far too few in number to handle a caseload. This means the new law may age significantly before it is allowed to affect market behavior. In the process it will lose credibility with the very people it is designed to affect.

An alternative to this "draft, implement, and enforce sequence" is the kind of focus strategy discussed earlier—to promote intermediated credit or direct markets, for example. Such a strategy gives a sequence to the content of the law and also to efforts to develop the legal process, by identifying where to start work and what is needed to implement and enforce the key laws. For example, the direct finance strategy requires that the government's capacity to implement the key financial laws be developed by drafting prudential and disclosure rules and training regulators to carry them out, designing administrative procedures for the process. Among commercial laws, the company law requires a registry for companies. Table 7-1 illustrates in matrix form the types of work necessary at each stage of the legal process.

Enforcement may need special attention with a direct finance strategy, particularly if investors are relied on to assert their rights. They must learn their rights, then have the resources and venues for action, with trained lawyers to help them. This is no small order, even if the principal shareholders in companies are mutual funds or other institutional investors. To create a judiciary capable of handling cases of this sort, the country may need to concentrate its judicial talent in courts devoted to commercial suits.

In summary, the matrix in table 7-1 shows the substantive laws and legal processes needed for a direct finance strategy. Sequencing is

TABLE 7-1. *Law and Legal Processes for a Direct Finance Strategy*

	Types of laws	
Stages of the legal process	*Financial laws*	*Commercial laws*
1. Legislative drafting	Laws for markets: securities, stock exchange, institutional investors	Constitution, company and contract laws; negotiable instruments and fiduciary laws (agency, trust)
2. Implementation	Prudential and disclosure rules, regulators, and systems	Company registry
3. Enforcement	Systems for investor self-enforcement commercial codes	

implicit. These take precedence over other laws and legal processes. But the matrix does not specify a sequence for the elements of substance and process in it that are required by the direct finance strategy; rather, all the elements should be present or take effect at about the same time. Because this would strain the resources of most transition countries, one could imagine this rough order:

—*Substantive laws:* constitution first, then contract law and company law for commerce generally, followed by securities law, stock exchange law, and negotiable instruments law, and finally by laws governing institutional investors.

—*Legal process:* drafting of laws first, then training for implementation and enforcement. After enactment of a sufficient body of laws, technical assistance is begun to help implement and enforce specific laws.

The limits of using this strategy to focus law development are most obvious at the enforcement stage. A reliance on commercial courts has ramifications throughout the legal system, applying to nonfinancial commercial transactions and siphoning resources from noncommercial areas of law. Family law and human rights are examples. Financial reform cannot drive judicial development alone, but working courts may be essential to the financial reforms in the long term. Now much judicial reform seems to be prompted by projects to change the political dynamic of the country, such as democratization. This must continue, but it is now time for economic considerations to play a role in the courts' development.

CONCLUSIONS

When financial reform is the primary focus of law development, greater attention to sequencing issues would be useful. Considered sequencing is rare in most transitional countries. But the financial reform strategy means other approaches are forgone. For example, a strategy built around the needs of the manufacturing or agricultural sector might lead to a different sequence of law development. It is not clear to me that the needs of the financial sector should predominate.

The goals of financial reform are a driving force, but they alone do not determine the sequence of law development. Broader economic and social goals inevitably help shape the context within which law development takes place. Five other key questions blending politics, economics, and law need to be answered before a country embarks on a course of reform and charts its priorities for legal development.

1. WHAT IS THE STATE OF THE COUNTRY'S FINANCIAL SYSTEM NOW? Is the country's financial system rudimentary, as in Kyrgyzstan? If so, the legal work starts with the basics. If the country's financial system is sophisticated, the sequence must be different. In the Czech Republic, where more than 1,000 companies are listed, the sequence of law development for the financial sector will be focused much more on particular problems than it would in Kyrgyzstan.[5]

2. HOW WILLING AND ABLE IS THE GOVERNMENT TO MOVE TO A MARKET ECONOMY? A "right-thinking" government with clout can push a coordinated legislative program through its parliament and deliver the laws intact. But what if the executive branch, however well intentioned, cannot deliver? What if a parliament tears apart draft laws? One may have to rethink the sequence. The content of the law development program may change. Suppose a mortgage law and land law are high on the list but the parliament will not pass them. One must simply put them on hold and proceed with other more acceptable laws.[6] The process certainly changes: either train legislators or work through the executive branch with a narrower agenda, perhaps substituting decrees for legislation. Decrees are easier to change than laws,

which has both good and bad consequences. Politics affects sequencing; law development is a political process.

A subquestion is how fast the government is willing to privatize. It is hard to get the attention of the executive branch regarding systems to implement a securities law if the government plans to have few companies with traded shares.

3. HOW WILLING IS THE GOVERNMENT TO RELY ON EXTERNAL SYSTEMS OF FINANCE AND LAW? The law adviser has a relatively easy job when working with a government that is open to foreign investment, has the prospects to attract foreign investment, and is willing to rely on foreign laws wherever possible. Here it is best to quickly decide among foreign legal systems or models that foreign investors find acceptable and adopt them. For example, foreign or international arbitration procedures may be adopted quickly.

But when a government wants to develop its own legal system fitted to domestic needs and not specifically to accommodate foreign investors, the sequence of work is different. The first item of law development is not the foreign investment code and the acceptance of treaties to resolve disputes with foreign investors.

4. WHAT METHOD DOES THE COUNTRY CURRENTLY USE TO RESOLVE ECONOMIC DISPUTES? Some countries settle business disputes mainly by social or economic means (like Japan). Others (like the United States) rely much more on legal institutions. This is not merely a stage of economic development; it is profoundly associated with a country's society. If reliance on social and economic sanctions is strong, the approach to law development and its sequencing must reflect this reality. Instead of detailed legislation, one may draft general propositions based on consensus, strengthen implementation, and downplay enforcement by the judiciary.

5. WHAT IS THE PREVAILING LEGAL SYSTEM IN THE COUNTRY? Many countries with a British colonial heritage use common law, building on the precedent of judicial decisions about individual cases. Many countries with a European colonial history use code law, stating general principles framed by statute. Former communist countries often superimposed a socialist code on the Western codes, some maintaining parts of the Western codes and others not. Some countries also rely on religious law (the Islamic countries are an example) or customary law.

One cannot draw simple prescriptions from the mere existence of one or the other system. The country may not want the prevailing legal system someday. The differences between common law and code law may be exaggerated now, particularly regarding finance. Common law countries have extensive statutory law for finance. Code law countries have often drafted special statutes for banking and other financial activities, independent of the codes.

That said, the legal system will influence the sequence of law development. A country with a code system may quickly need certain work that a common law country does not need; for example, code law countries need trust law. A country with developed neighbors using code law will probably want a code system to ease cross-border trade and investment. The needs of the codes shape the sequence of law development. Eastern European countries probably fit in with this group better than with those countries in Central Asia.

Of these questions, only one is strictly for lawyers, and it is the last. It is important, but many of the answers to the other questions will have to come from nonlawyers. Their responses should set the parameters for law development and sequencing. However, I fear that often nonlawyers play only a minor role in law development. This is a serious problem that needs attention.

REFERENCES

Durkheim, Émile. 1984. *The Division of Labor*. Free Press.
La Porta, Rafael, and others. 1996. "Law and Finance." Working Paper 5661. Cambridge, Mass.: National Bureau of Economic Research (July).
North, Douglass Cecil. 1990. *Institutions, Institutional Change, and Economic Performance*. Cambridge University Press.
Shipton, Parker, Robert Vogel, and Philip Wellons. 1995. "Financial Reform: A Manual for Assessing the Roles of Law and Culture." Discussion Paper No. 33. Cambridge, Mass.: Harvard Institute for International Development, Consultants and Assistants on Economic Reform (March).
Upham, Frank. 1986. "Legal and Institutional Dynamics in Japan's Cartel Policy." In *Japan's Response to Crisis and Change in the World Economy*, edited by A. Schmiegelow. Armonk, N.Y.: Sharpe.

Weber, Max. 1984 (originally published 1950). *General Economic History (1919–1920)*. Glencoe, Ill.: Free Press.

World Bank. 1989. *World Development Report*. Washington.

NOTES

1. For an explanation of the relevance of law to financial sector development, see World Bank (1989).

2. A more complete elaboration of these elements, with detailed examples, can be found in Shipton, Vogel, and Wellons (1995).

3. The classic view appears in Weber (1984/1950); Durkheim (1984). A more recent version is North (1990).

4. See, for example, Upham (1986).

5. Although no study relates law to the state of a country's financial system, a recent study found a complicated relationship between law and per capita income, an indicator of development. The sophistication of financial systems is often a function of the complexity of the economy. In a sample of more than forty countries, the higher a country's per capita income, the more effective enforcement proved to be, particularly in the improved capacity of the judiciary. On the other hand, certain creditors' rights became less effective, and no relationship was found regarding shareholders' rights. See La Porta and others (1996).

6. *Law and Finance* reported that to some extent laws, at least for investor protection, can substitute for one another. For example, mandatory dividends may protect shareholders when fiduciary laws governing managers fail to do so.

Chapter 8

BETTY F. SLADE

Coordinating Prudential Regulations: A Multisector Approach

The important role of prudential regulation in financial reform was recognized late in the discussion of the benefits liberalization of financial systems has for developing countries. The early books of McKinnon and Shaw discussing financial repression and liberalization made no mention of prudential regulation.[1] Serious discussion of the topic as an important element of financial reform began in the mid-1980s; today, the implementation of prudential regulation is widely seen as integral to the financial reform process. Even the sequencing literature seems to take for granted that prudential regulation is necessary, but often without detailed elaboration.[2]

A careful look at prudential regulation in financial reform came in 1984 when U.S. Federal Reserve Governor Wallich observed, "We need to look closely at the whys of financial regulation not in the spirit of 'give-it-a-fair-trial-and-hang-it,' but of giving the devil his due. . . . Regulation gives 'safety'. . . . It is not easy to make a dedicated official understand that the activity to which he has devoted his career damages the economy. . . . But deregulation leads to additional risks. Greater risks from deregulation can be countered by appropriate supervisory action."[3]

Economists Cargill, Sheng, and Hutchison went on to observe in 1986: "The new regulatory approach has brought with it . . . old regulatory problems in a new market setting: risk to individual financial institutions, stability of the whole financial system, depositor protection and prevention of financial panics, clash between role of government financial intermediation and private intermediation, selective credit allocation policies, issues for monetary policy."[4]

Maxwell Fry suggested in 1988 that "successful financial liberalization depends on macroeconomic stability and adequate bank supervison."[5] In the same year Cole and I stated: "A supervisory and regulatory system oriented to asset quality and measures of liquidity and solvency must replace a system primarily concerned with following bureaucratic directives as to prices and credit allocation. All these changes not only take time, but also often require a change in leadership or, at least, in attitude of those directing key institutions."[6]

A conference held at Cambridge in June 1990 put considerable emphasis on prudential regulation. As summed up by Vittas, "new rules of the game have been made that govern operations of financial institutions and markets from controls and restrictions to prudential and investor protection regulations."[7] In 1991, Sundararajan and Balino emphasized that sound prudential policies and their proper enforcement are critical in minimizing major disruptions to growth and stability.[8]

Proper sequencing of financial reform requires that core prudential regulations be introduced early on in the liberalization process and that the political will to enforce them be present. Practically speaking, there is likely to be a lag between the political opportunities to introduce reform and the adoption of comprehensive prudential regulations. The expertise and institutional framework to develop and implement detailed regulations may not initially exist. Nor will the need appear critical to politicians until more experience has been gained with liberalized financial markets. But policymakers must be kept aware of the activities and developments within the financial sector. To achieve this, it is necessary that the various financial sector activities be monitored and continuously evaluated. In many cases this early responsibility falls on those institutions likely to become the key prudential regulators—for example, the central bank and the ministry of finance, or their equivalents. Therefore, the prudential regulators should be key participants in the discussion of financial policy issues early on. The central bankers and finance ministers often do not think of themselves as regulators when present at the relevant meetings.

Another important problem is the lack of coordination among various agencies that have some role in the regulatory process; increased coordination should be a cornerstone of prudential regulatory policy. The need for such coordination is similar to the customary calls for coordination in monetary and fiscal policies, exchange rate, and balance of payments policies. An important step is that regulators representing the various financial sectors should have a forum to discuss issues with policymakers. A key purpose of early discussions would be to keep policymakers informed of the progress toward effective, prudential regulation. Financial reform often takes place in response to some type of crisis, so it is appropriate that politicians and policymakers have some grasp of the situation when they are forced to act.

RECONCILING THE GOALS OF LIBERALIZATION AND PRUDENTIAL REGULATIONS

Two important characteristics of market-oriented financial systems in the transition from government-controlled systems are increased efficiency and increased risk of institutional failure. A main goal of prudential regulation is to lower the risks and costs associated with institutional failure, while achieving the increased efficiency of the financial system. Because prudential regulation addresses this central problem, it should be considered an integral component of financial reform and economic liberalization. Liberalization should not be considered by government to be a hands-off endeavor. Government should maintain a role to ensure fair and honest markets, but prudential regulations should not be used to continue previous bureaucratic controls or to weaken market discipline. Market-based financial discipline should be allowed to provide the correct signals and constraints to encourage borrowers and lenders to act in accord with their risk and return preferences. The harsh discipline of the market will inevitably entail failed institutions, but appropriate regulation can help ensure that this process takes place in an orderly fashion and with acceptable costs.

Certain measures associated with prudential regulation should be initiated early in the process to help in achieving the goals of financial reform. As I have noted, core prudential regulations (along with the liberalization measures themselves) should be identified and issued insofar as possible. Efforts should be made during that process to consult with private sector experts and market participants to better understand how markets to be regulated actually function. An important feature is cooperation among regulators of the various types of financial institutions and activities. Regulatory authorities from the start should systematically collect, monitor, and publish data that can be released to the public. Release of such information can help overcome the problem of asymmetric information and ensure public confidence and understanding as the reform process is implemented.

Cooperation

Prudential regulators can coordinate their efforts in different ways, either formally or informally, depending on the circumstances of the particular country. But as a general rule, meetings should be held regularly and a formal cooperative body established. The goals of cooperation among agencies include preventing gaps in prudential authority; clarifying authority for regulation of functions that cross over traditional market classifications, such as brokerage activities by banks, pension, and investment fund custodial activities of banks; defining the authority of market professionals, such as lawyers, accountants, and auditors; preventing unnecessary conflicts among the various regulatory agencies; resolving conflicts between the central bank, the ministry of finance, and other relevant government agencies; and maintaining an overview of the system so that regulators can act together in a major crisis.

Regulators of financial services have been drawing closer to each other at the international level than at the national level. It has been recognized that innovations in the delivery of financial services and globalizing trends have weakened the performance of national financial institutions and exposed gaps in regulatory regimes.[9] To deal with these weaknesses, the Basel Committee on Banking Supervision has proposed risk-weighted capital adequacy standards. The Technical Committee of the International Organization of Securities Commissions (IOSCO) has also been working to harmonize the capital requirements of banks and securities companies and has worked in cooperation with the Basel Committee. World securities market regulators met in October 1994 and adopted a resolution on basic principles for uniform regulatory standards and mutual cooperation and assistance among nations. Their final communiqué called for joint work with the Bank for International Settlements (BIS) on regulation of over-the-counter derivatives.[10] But problems remain in such areas as risks in payments, clearing, and settlement systems and gaps in supervision of bank foreign activities. Attempts at such international initiatives underscore the need for cooperation among separate regulatory agencies within countries.

High-Level Oversight Body

Countries can encourage and formalize cooperation among regulators by setting up a high-level oversight body consisting of top regulators and key policymakers to review the issues and proposed regulations. This entity should probably have its own permanent expert staff. There are practical problems in creating such an entity, but the role it could serve would be an important one, particularly in the early years of liberalization. Requiring that prudential regulators report on their efforts to the oversight body can instill discipline in their organizations that might not otherwise exist and could foster a useful dialogue between policymakers and regulators.

Because of interagency rivalries, interagency discussion tends to be minimal in many countries except in times of crisis. For example, bank regulators often have higher status and pay and better positions than other financial regulators. Heavy responsibilities and a lack of expertise that creates defensiveness can also thwart cooperation. There are certain areas in which oversight and review are especially important.

ESTABLISHING THE NECESSARY LEGAL BASES FOR REGULATIONS IS A CRITICAL TASK FOR THE OVERSIGHT BODY AND POLICY OFFICIALS. The legal framework is a combination of regulatory and policy principles clearly set forth in operating documents, which specifies the means to implement and enforce the general principles. The legal framework will include laws, government regulations, decrees, and circulars, as well as ad hoc rules and directives, and will establish a clear hierarchy of law. The legal rules need to be organized, internally consistent, and readily available to the public. Laws should have clear enforcement provisions and indicate the responsibilities and roles of regulators and other market professionals such as lawyers, accountants, appraisers, actuaries, and auditors. Establishing an effective legal framework for prudential regulation has proven to be extremely difficult in practice and needs strong and continual policy attention.

THE OVERSIGHT BODY SHOULD CONSIDER THE ISSUE OF WHETHER REGULATORY AUTHORITY SHOULD BE HIGHLY CENTRALIZED OR DECENTRALIZED. Should authority be combined in one organization, with a series of functional divisions? Should it be a series of institutions with no direct relationship among them? Or is something in between a highly centralized or a highly decentralized structure called for? Often regulatory authority is segmented according to type of institution. Separate regulatory agencies are frequently encountered for banks, insurance, and certain capital market institutions. In the early years of liberalization, regulation of multifinance companies, other deposit-taking institutions, and pension funds often are neglected or assigned to weak institutions. In the United States, for example, pension fund activities are still only weakly regulated. Derivatives and other new cross-national and cross-sector activities have been poorly understood and have been unregulated. Differences between banks and nonbank regulation have to some extent been the result of historical circumstances within each country, as financial sectors have grown unevenly and governments have responded differently. However, countries often neglect the prudential regulation of certain kinds of financial activities.

Goals also differ among various regulatory agencies. As a practical matter, some separation of authority among regulatory entities has been recogized as efficient and has been the trend throughout the world. However, in some countries, consideration might be given to a more centralized regulatory system, especially in cases where prudential regulation has grown up haphazardly in response to specific needs and as a result lacks coherence. A case in point is the overlapping and hugely complex banking regulatory structure in the United States. In other cases, more checks and balances, pluralism, and specialization of regulatory functions are needed. For example, the banking system dominates the economy in many countries in the early stages of financial development. Banking regulators may aggrandize their role by taking on regulatory functions for other sectors of finance as they began to emerge. The Malaysian central bank took on most regulatory functions as the various new financial sectors developed. In recent years it has begun to divest these functions into other agencies.

CORE REGULATIONS IDEALLY SHOULD BE ISSUED ALONG WITH THE LIBERALIZATION PACKAGE OR FOLLOW IT CLOSELY. Opinions differ as to what should be included in a basic set of regulations that make up the "core," and these must be resolved early in the liberalization process. Although core regulations might be considered different for various countries, some areas that should normally be included in such a list are entry and exit criteria, capital standards, portfolio diversification standards, accurate reporting requirements, insider trading and manipulative prohibitions, the nature and types of supervision, and enforcement mechanisms. There is extensive international experience in these areas that countries can draw on, and the oversight body should focus efforts on the need for core regulations at an early stage.

Prudential regulatory agencies organized to deal with different functions would naturally have quite different priorities and goals. For example, banking regulators will address liquidity, solvency, and safety of the individual bank, while policymakers worry about the potential of these banks to undermine the payments system as a whole. Banking regulations tend to be comprehensive. Capital market regulations, as in the United States, may merely emphasize that sufficient information be made available to protect small investors and to prevent fraud. Pension and insurance regulators seek to protect the public against false promises that could undermine retirement benefits or the ability to recover losses in the future. In some cases, the regulation is simply to ensure that financial institutions or venture capital companies meet the legal requirements under which they were established. Governments also frequently use prudential rules to protect against private anticompetitive behavior. Given the different goals of the regulators, regulatory gaps may arise, with the result that economic activity moves from the more regulated to the less regulated sectors. The oversight body, if it has full information, would monitor these developments and focus efforts on emerging needs.

At the implementation level there are several significant administrative issues. Often the effectiveness of prudential regulation varies significantly from sector to sector because of the more successful management techniques and administrative leadership in certain sectors. The oversight body should evaluate the practical effectiveness of the various regulatory bodies in terms of specific managerial issues—for example, quality of offsite reporting and early warning systems; onsite examination; self-regulation; and training of auditors, bank examiners, and other professionals. An oversight body should recognize gaps and overlapping jurisdiction and should evaluate the administrative capacities of agencies through periodic reports. In case of overlap, decisions could be made regarding which regulatory authority should have major responsibility. An example of this is the regulation of brokers and dealers who are members of the U.S. NASDAQ system versus regulation by one or more of the major exchanges. In many cases, the National Association of Securities Dealers (NASD) is given responsibility for oversight of these brokers and dealers, who would have to expect examinations several times a year—a costly and disruptive process. Gaps can be recognized when it becomes clear that some financial institutions or functions within them are not subject to any prudential oversight.

It must be recognized that qualified prudential regulators are a scarce commodity and are frequent targets of bribery. Prudential regulators need to enjoy high status and remuneration but must be expected to maintain impeccable standards. Remuneration of staff among regulatory agencies often varies widely. For example, central bank regulators are frequently better paid than capital market regulators simply because of their organization's status. There should be a mutual interest among regulators that their organizations all have qualified and adequately paid staff. The oversight body should ensure that proper standards are set for regulators, addressing the issues of status, pay, training, and standards of conduct of regulatory officials. Codes of ethics and standards for professional organizations usually are not standard for the various financial sectors; in fact, such codes may not exist at all. These standards should be required for foreign exchange and money market brokers, securities brokers and dealers, stock exchanges, clearing corporations, and professional associations for lawyers, accountants, appraisers, auditors, and actuaries. Something else that needs to be considered is that regulators suffer from low morale when their activities are not supported by policymakers. Their attempts to enforce regulations typically meet with resistance from powerful interests, and their morale is particularly influenced by the level of support they receive. The oversight body can help provide such support.

ONE OF THE MAJOR OBSTACLES TO THE PROPER FUNCTIONING OF THE MARKET MECHANISM IS THE PROBLEM OF ASYMMETRIC AND UNRELIABLE INFORMATION. The party with special access to information has an advantage over others and can use it in a financial transaction. Lenders, for example, should have access to relevant information. Off–balance sheet liabilities, such as loan guarantees, make it difficult to determine how these liabilities should be regarded in assessing a borrower's or a bank's total indebtedness. Prudential regulatory agencies can provide much useful information to one another and to the attentive public. Regulatory agencies are often reluctant to release information, even in a highly consolidated form. However, widely disseminated and reliable information is critical to investment decisions and to the normal operations of all financial markets.

ALL TOO OFTEN THERE ARE NO PLANS TO MEET EMERGENCY SITUATIONS, EVEN THOUGH ALL COUNTRIES FACE SIMILAR CRISES FROM TIME TO TIME. The oversight body should take the initiative to develop emergency plans in case of financial crises. This should be one of its major responsibilities.

Effective prudential regulation requires functioning institutions with appropriate record-keeping and effective management. A central issue in the move from direct controls to market-based operations is an effective institutional framework in the various markets. Government or government-related agencies should assist in setting up market-supporting institutions and professional standards in each financial sector. In most cases, the government (in some form) must take the initiative for private development of market supervisory mechanisms, or at least not stifle it. Prudential regulations are sometimes inappropriately viewed as a means to promote equity or otherwise to affect allocation of credit. The intervention to promote equity generally backfires, even though it is well-meaning. But at the same time, governments must not allow their regulatory systems to be captured by powerful groups who want to perpetuate their own monopoly positions and access to capital.

WHEN LIBERALIZATION PRECEDES PRUDENTIAL REGULATIONS: INDONESIA

Examples from Indonesian experience reinforce the message that prudential regulatory measures should accompany liberalization. The

1983 Income Tax Law made contributions to and income from private pension funds tax free; no law or prudential rules for private pension funds were enacted concurrently. Some pension funds became unrestricted tax-free sources of funds for employers. The Pension Fund Law was passed only in 1992, and regulatory authority was given to the Ministry of Finance. The Indonesian government allowed the capital market to open up rapidly in 1988–90. As the government adopted a hands-off attitude, serious problems of disclosure, manipulation, and legal gaps arose. The Ministry of Finance then issued a comprehensive capital market prudential policy in December 1990. A capital market law was finally passed in early 1996. The earlier prudential rules slowed the explosive growth of the Indonesian capital market, probably preventing a panic or financial crisis similar to those experienced in other Asian countries.

In October 1988, the Indonesian government freed up entry and other aspects of banking. The monetary authorities took a casual attitude toward rapid credit expansion and monetary growth from 1989 through mid-1990. The central bank mainly tried to push down interest rates. As a consequence of the government policy, banks expanded too rapidly and engaged in risky activities. Several banks got into trouble through mismanagement and excessive risk taking. An ill-suited set of prudential requirements was issued by the central bank in February 1991 but revised in May 1993. Since then, the system of bank supervision has improved. Most private banks have responded to the increased pressure from the central bank and have sought to conform to the new rules. State banks have been forced to comply by a special joint government committee of finance and central bank officials who have strong backing from top officials.

Although it may be argued that Indonesia acted when necessary to correct the defects in its financial system, it is more cogent to conclude that resorting sooner to the more modest prudential regulations that have since been adopted would have averted serious problems without stifling the growth of the economy or financial markets. In general, better coordination and a reduced time lag between liberalization and imposition of appropriate prudential regulations would have been preferable for the development of the Indonesian financial system, but political realities will invariably affect the timing of and the possibilities for such steps.

REFERENCES

Cheng, Hang-Sheng. 1986. *Financial Policy and Reform in Pacific Basin Countries.* Lexington, Mass.: D. C. Heath/Lexington Books.

Cole, David C., and Betty F. Slade-Yaser. 1988. "Reform of Financial Systems." Paper prepared for the HIID Conference on Systems Reform in Developing Countries, Marrakesh, Morocco (October). Later published in Perkins, Dwight H., and Michael Roemer, eds. *Reforming Economic Systems in Developing Countries.* 1991. Harvard University Press.

Fry, Maxwell. 1988. *Money, Interest and Banking in Economic Development.* Johns Hopkins University Press.

Goldstein, Morris , and others. 1992. *International Capital Markets Developments, Prospects and Policy Issues.* Washington: International Monetary Fund (September).

McKinnon, Ronald I. 1973. *Money and Capital in International Development.* Brookings.

———. 1989. "Macroeconomic Instability and Moral Hazard in a Liberalizing Economy." In *Latin American Debt and Adjustment: External Shocks and Macroeconomic Policies,* edited by Philip L. Broh, Michael B. Connolly, and Claudio Gonzalez-Vega, 99–111. Praeger.

Shaw, Edward. 1973. *Financial Deepening and Economic Development.* Oxford University Press.

Sundararajan, Vasudeva, and Tomás J. T. Baliño. 1991. *Banking Crises: Cases and Issues.* Washington: International Monetary Fund.

Vittas, Dimitri, ed. 1992. *Financial Regulation: Changing the Rules of the Game.* Washington: EDI Development Series.

"World Regulators Agree to Address Problem of 'Uncooperative' Markets." 1994. *Indonesian Observer* (October 24).

NOTES

1. Shaw (1973); McKinnon (1973).

2. For example, McKinnon (1989) reflects underlying assumptions about prudential regulation, but does not address the issue in specific terms.

3. Cheng (1986, pp. 1–12).

4. Cheng (1986, p. 28).

5. Fry (1988, p. 425).

6. Cole and Slade-Yaser (1988, p. 56).

7. Vittas (1992, p. 1).

8. Sundararajan and Baliño (1991).

9. Goldstein and others (1992, p. 10).

10. "World Regulators Agree to Address Problem of 'Uncooperative' Markets" (1994).

Chapter 9

GERARD CAPRIO, JR.

Bank Regulation: The Case of the Missing Model

Financial reforms of one type or another have been of growing importance since the appearance of McKinnon's seminal volume.[1] However,
disappointment with the fruits of this reform process is common,
especially in Africa and in transitional economies, perhaps in part
because of the reformers' high expectations. Disappointment with
reform measures may also be the result of perverse sequencing: Often
the more visible aspects of reform, such as complete interest rate
deregulation, bank recapitalization, or (more recently) the creation of
stock exchanges, have been pursued before the basic financial sector
infrastructure—auditing, accounting, legal systems, and basic regulations—is in place.[2] In this chapter I focus on the basic infrastructure
and argue that the overall regulatory framework must be attuned to
the institutional structure of the economy and encourage prudent
behavior, to contribute to the overall success of financial sector reforms. Moreover, because participants in the financial system, both
individuals and organizations, take time to adjust to changes in incentives, it is important to design and implement changes in the regulatory environment early in the reform process.

Why are regulatory changes—along with other financial reforms—
difficult to design, implement, enforce, and evaluate? In the next section I address this question, contending that there are many problems
with current popular regulatory approaches in both industrial and
developing countries, which put supervision as the first line of defense against unsafe and unsound banking practices. In the third
section I lay out possible options for building safer, sounder banking
systems and argue that a fundamental element in any positive change
should include aligning incentives of bank owners with the goals of
the country and the national authorities (that is, making the system

"incentive compatible"). These goals should include the mobilization of savings and their efficient and prudent allocation. The options for better banking include letting depositors have more of their funds at risk (a form of coinsurance), mandating or inducing (through higher liability limits) significantly higher capital adequacy ratios above those recommended by the Basel Committee, narrow banking, stricter entry limits to reduce competition in some financial systems, free banking, and mandatory diversification ratios. Enhanced supervision, which would complement all of these options except for free banking, would occupy a supporting role, as it did in most countries before the 1930s.

Authorities in developing and transitional countries increasingly are following what might be called the Organization for Economic Cooperation and Development (OECD)-standard regulatory model: 8 percent risk-adjusted capital adequacy ratios and enhanced supervision, along with implicit or explicit deposit insurance. The proposals suggested here, in contrast, are radical and leave me open to being thought unrealistic. Perhaps the best response to these concerns is that if a new model is not considered now, when large losses have been sustained in developing and industrial economies, these considerations will be more realistic after the next wave of crises, when still larger losses can be expected. For some countries where the losses have already been quite large (including Japan, Mexico, and Venezuela) or the injections of capital repeated (such as in Hungary), the future might be now.

WHY ARE REGULATORY CHANGES SO DIFFICULT?

Why are financial reforms, including regulatory changes, so difficult to put in place? First, there is no simple index of successful financial reform. As noted by Levine in chapter 2 of this book, finance performs a variety of functions, many of which are difficult to measure. Even if one were to confine the analysis to changes in banking, the indicators that are readily available—banks' balance sheet and income statements—are subject to a variety of reporting differences within and across countries. As a result, they can be manipulated to show what owners would like them to convey. For example, as illustrated by de

Juan, the easiest way to improve how good a given loan looks is by granting another loan to the same borrower: the practice of "evergreening."[3] De Juan also illustrated clearly how banks that are in trouble—often because of insufficient diversification or interest or exchange rate mismatches—can in effect build their balance sheet and income statement from the bottom up (for example, beginning first with the dividends they think are necessary to pay and arriving later at the interest income needed to justify the given dividend). With this amount of freedom, depositors, shareholders, and even supervisors will have a difficult time evaluating a bank's condition. Only recently and only in a few developing countries have firm-level data become available. These data permit the assessment of how the allocation of capital has changed and, by implication, how the banking system is performing one of its key roles, but this analysis does not elucidate the performance of individual banks.[4]

A variety of factors, many of which are difficult to quantify, complicate the task of assessing reform impacts. Although many have argued that the impact of financial reforms will depend on macroeconomic factors, this reasoning often assumed that finance is unimportant and only passively reflects the workings of macroeconomics. Gertler and Rose instead cast the argument in a new framework. They assume information asymmetries and then reach the conclusion that, in such an environment, lending decisions will significantly depend on borrower net worth.[5] Shocks that reduce borrower net worth will drive up the premium for external finance and reduce investment, thereby potentially impairing intermediaries. Regulatory changes at times of improving borrower net worth will appear judicious, even if they entail significant future costs; those preceding a collapse of borrower net worth will tend to be labeled failures, regardless of their merit. Given the crucial dependence of reforms and regulatory changes on borrower net worth, it would appear sensible to wait several business cycles before drawing firm conclusions about the success of any changes.[6]

In addition to borrower net worth, the impact of reforms affecting the banking system depends on a variety of conditions at the outset, including the initial balance sheet and how it is allocated, the endowment of information and human capital, and most important, the incentive systems in financial intermediaries.[7] Although reform programs often take account of the starting balance sheet, usually the focus is only on whether the bank begins with positive or negative net worth. Certainly, net worth is an important variable. But attention paid to this variable has biased reforms toward assuming that once any solvency problems have been fixed, little else need be done to ensure that banks will operate in a safe and sound manner. Yet the allocation of assets matters importantly as well: a skewed balance sheet before reform can lead to rapid reallocations as constraints are eased. Simultaneous portfolio reallocation by an entire banking system can produce swings in asset prices that have the potential to be destabilizing, as can be seen in cases as diverse as those associated with housing and land price bubbles in Scandinavia, Japan, and Malaysia.[8]

But even when these balance sheet variables are taken into account, other initial conditions can lead to postreform problems. If banks have information primarily about unprofitable sectors, then they will tend either to continue lending to businesses they understand (even if those are unprofitable) or to underinvest in what they see as risky projects. The former case could be expected, for example, when state-owned banks in a transitional economy are accustomed to dealing with (or compelled to continue lending to) state-owned enterprises, or perhaps when private banks that have already gone bust undertake to lend to high-risk clients. In this case they might be willing to lend at high interest rates based on the (small) chance that the client might be able to repay and thereby rescue the bank from insolvency. When banks are solvent and profit-maximizing, they tend to retreat from lending when information capital is depleted. This is especially so when accounting and auditing standards, the basis for much financial information, are underdeveloped.[9]

Weak human capital, a routine feature of banking systems emerging from a long period of repression, can also tend to exhaust even substantial capital holdings—a reason, it should be clear, why significantly high capital ratios are not sufficient to ensure safe and sound banking. But even more pernicious is the incentive system in banks following prolonged repression. To the extent that it reflects the preform environment, which may have emphasized lending to unprofitable activities, the incentive system can continue to distort the allocation of capital long after reforms have been instituted. If the incentive system favors lending regardless of return, or acting like an employment agency rather than a bank, turning the organization around will be difficult without significant change, most likely including some change of ownership. State-owned banks are particularly difficult to change, as profits are not their final goal and (at least in most state-owned banks with which I am familiar) compensation differentials are compressed and are not used to motivate staff.[10]

One popular example of slow-changing banking incentives is the U.S. case after introduction of federal deposit insurance. Although this reform, enacted in 1933, might have been expected to lead to more risk taking on the part of bankers, in fact for the next 20 to 30 years, bankers—those who lived through the many banking failures of the 1920s and 1930s—remained quite conservative. It was only as non-banks began to make significant competitive inroads into the banking business (resulting in lower financial value) and as the Depression-era bankers retired that "go-go" banking became popular.[11] Reforms might be expected to lead to more rapid changes where such significant shocks are absent and where the banking system is in private hands. State-owned banks tend to be much less responsive, if at all, to economic forces induced by reforms. As a result, they might be expected to be the slowest to change.

Regulations are an important part of the initial conditions. They are effectively one of the most important variables external to banks that help determine, with some lag, their internal incentive systems. For this reason, and because variations in regulations can take time to influence these incentive systems (and eventually bank performance), it appears sensible to strive for regulatory change early in the reform process. The logic of this proposed sequencing is even clearer when supervision is initially weak: It will then be especially important to align incentives for bank owners and managers with the goals of the financial system.

Most explicit or implicit models of banking regulation and supervision—certainly those in virtually every OECD country today, with the notable exception of New Zealand—assume an important role for bank supervision by both government and bank supervisors.[12] The popularity of bank supervision likely results from a misreading of the post–World War II experience of the United States. In fact, largely because of political resistance to the emergence of truly national banks, the U.S. banking system historically has been relatively weak. Where there are so many banks—30,000 in the United States in the early 1920s, versus about 11,000 today—and (at least in part) as a result so many bank failures, it is no wonder that supervision has been considered necessary.

Effective bank supervision is important for the developing and transitional economies, because their prereform system merely verified compliance with regulations regarding direction of credit. Supervision can provide a credible threat that unsound or fraudulent activities will be detected and punished. However, it is difficult to believe that supervision can ever serve as the first line of defense against unsafe, unsound banking. Consider, for example, Rolnick's argument that it would be easy for bankers to hop on a plane to Las Vegas and put their entire assets at risk on the roulette wheel.[13] With limited liability, it is trivial for bankers to hedge this risk and to wind up at least no worse off than before, and possibly a good deal richer. Deposit insurance, either implicit or explicit, provides bankers with the incentive to engage in such behavior if they are not highly rewarded for taking prudent risks.[14] After all, they can always try to move elsewhere and try again. Only the taxpayer ends up worse off, in effect blindly underwriting risk taking that most (except for the casino owners) would not knowingly endorse. Although this is admittedly a contrived example, it illustrates that, at least in some cases, by the time supervisors or depositors find out about a problem, the bank will have already lost all of its capital.

In addition to the possibility of fleet-footed bankers, supervision suffers in many countries, because it is difficult to train and retain highly competent supervisors. Skilled supervisors will likely earn much more from private financial intermediaries and will have strong incentives to leave once having attained competent performance levels. In additon, like many generals, supervisors have a tendency to fight the last war. U.S. and Japanese bank supervisors, for example, are alert to overlending to the real estate sector or to developing countries, but are less prepared for problems from new risks, such as those posed by derivatives.[15]

Moreover, even when supervisors know of a situation sufficiently early to prevent large losses, political forces may prevent them from acting. In Chile, supervisors maintained that they knew that bankers were not covering their exchange risk, but they were prevented from requiring it because a fixed exchange rate was government policy. More blatant cases of abusing political power, such as the attempt by U.S. savings and loan (S&L) executives to buy congressional influence and regulatory forbearance, are all too common. In Venezuela, according to the former head of the National Securities Commission, the problems at Banco Latino, a "rogue" bank, were known as early as 1992, though the bank was not closed until January 1994. However, losses began mounting rapidly in 1992, and the bank had already lost its capital by that point, having made poor credit decisions—such as bidding up deposit rates—for some time.[16] Nonetheless, by the time it was finally closed in early 1994, Banco Latino's behavior had already spread to other banks. It was estimated that in late 1994 seventeen of Venezuela's fifty banks were in critical condition, and others were receiving extensive government support.[17] Inflation has since soared, and capital flight has been associated with an approximate 50 percent fall in the value of the bolivar.

Strengthening supervision will be an arduous task, and there is no guaranteed path to a safe and sound banking system. Experienced supervisors estimate that it could take many countries five to ten years of substantial training before their supervisors' skills would be near the capacity found in industrial countries. Even if supervision were the secret to better banking, does it make sense for countries starved of human capital to allocate significant talent to supervising banks?

The preceding comments are not meant to suggest that supervision is unimportant. Good bank supervisors can be an effective ally for bank owners and senior management, helping to send a credible signal that fraud and unsafe practices will be punished. Transforming bank supervision from a system of checking on compliance with credit directives to one aimed at encouraging prudent risk taking is an important effort in this regard. But the point here is that without motivated owners, bank supervision alone will probably be ineffective.

WHAT ARE THE OPTIONS FOR BETTER BANKING?

For the reasons I have just discussed, the OECD model, based on enhanced supervision and an 8 percent risk-adjusted capital ratio, is not likely to be adequate for developing and transitional economies. There are several options that are likely to prove more fruitful. Their common theme is to improve in one way or another the incentives facing bankers.

The first option calls for increased monitoring of banks by depositors by a complete or partial end to deposit insurance. The advantage is that depositors with funds at risk have the incentive to invest effort in investigating banks; the possibility that they might move their funds to better banks would thus provide some incentive for bankers to behave more prudently. However, one important drawback is that banks are inherently opaque institutions, and depositors' ability to monitor them effectively can easily be doubted. Before deposit insurance, it was probably true that more resources were invested in unearthing information about banks. For example, in the United States during the Free Banking era, "Bank Note Monitors" existed as daily periodicals to review the safety of various banks. There is every reason to believe that new information sources would appear if depositor funds were at risk.

However, it is unclear that great weight should be placed on the shoulders of depositors, in view of the inability of even well-informed shareholders—and, with no safety net, presumably even those who are highly motivated—to successfully anticipate and predict bank failures.[18] Shareholders have access to substantial information already; the recommendation might therefore be to put at risk only limited depositor funds. Countries often only seek to provide insurance for small depositors, as larger depositors are thought to be better informed and able to take more steps to evaluate intermediaries. However, it makes little sense to make large depositors feel more exposed to risk. They might run at the first scent of real or imagined trouble, increasing system instability.[19] Moreover, large depositors can always divide their funds into smaller amounts or move accounts offshore, where full insurance might be provided. Historically, at least in the U.S. case, deposit insurance limits have grown because of political forces, so a strategy based on limiting deposit insurance to small depositors may be destined to erode over time.[20]

A more promising variant of this option, though one that remains vulnerable to this last criticism, is to provide a coinsurance fund, such as putting 20 percent of each depositor's account at risk.[21] This has the advantage of increasing depositor monitoring without making depositors too nervous. Moreover, the entire deposit is less at risk when there is a better chance of being able to monitor the risk effectively.

A second option to improve banking regulation, which could complement the first, is to require higher capital-asset ratios for bankers. Higher capital in theory gives depositors, shareholders, and supervisors more time to detect unsafe practices. As a result, it increases the motivation of owners to do so as well, as they will have more of their own funds to protect. As supervisors point out, however, the first fallback for problem loans is provisions and earnings, not capital.[22] Indeed, if bankers were motivated to provision aggressively, little capital might be required. Although German and U.S. banks in the nineteenth century routinely held capital ratios as high as 25 to 50 percent, merely mandating higher capital alone might not be sufficient. Indeed, the nineteenth-century practice of holding more capital was not attained by regulatory fiat, but resulted at least partly from the need to assure depositors (that is, noteholders) that their funds were safe.

A bank determined to take significant risks can exhaust its capital rapidly, as in the case of Rolnick's hypothetical casino example that I noted. Where supervisory skills are in short supply, raising capital ratios might comfort authorities and the public more, but it would not appear to be a first-best choice by itself. As with attempts to limit deposit insurance, high capital ratios might be impractical in a world of rapid communications, where banks can move readily offshore to havens with lower capital requirements. Although some governments—especially those which have just engaged in a costly bailout of the banking system—might be willing to see their banking industry move offshore, most will not tolerate this shift.

Rather than mandating higher capital ratios, then, a related variant that is appealing (especially given the difficulty in deciding what ratio is sufficient) is to raise liability limits on bank shareholders. In the United States before the 1920s, bank shareholders faced double liability in many states. This meant that if the bank's losses exhausted funds put up as capital, then the personal fortunes of shareholders were liable for a postclosure assessment up to the sum of funds they invested, respectively. Even more severe, during the Scottish Free Banking Era (roughly 1700–1844), bankers faced unlimited liability; not surprisingly, this appears to have been a time of highly prudent banking. Of course, it is possible to raise the penalty for risk taking so much that many prudent investments, which would produce faster growth, will not be undertaken.[23] Unfortunately, there has been little variation of regulatory practice concerning limits on the liability of bank shareholders to permit an empirical analysis regarding optimal levels. Without such knowledge, authorities who might consider experimenting might try raising liability limits to 150 or 200 percent, to see if this produces a desired change in banking practice without excessively choking off the supply of risk capital.[24] A variant of this idea is, in effect, to raise liability through a system of mutual liability, such as in the U.S. clearinghouse system, wherein member banks were liable for one another's losses. This system encouraged close supervision of member bank activities and appears to work well as long as membership in the system remains relatively small.[25]

A third option—one that has enjoyed some popularity in the United States—is the narrow banking model.[26] Banks would only be allowed to invest in safe instruments, such as government paper, while other institutions not insured by the government would be free to engage in riskier activities. Banks then would be failure-proof, or (if allowed to hold high-quality and highly liquid nongovernment paper) at least quite safe. Deposit guarantees would not likely be needed, as all risky activities would migrate to nonbank financial intermediaries. This proposal was made in the 1930s, long before the 1980s boom in mutual funds. Supporters often point to the desirable risk-sharing properties of this approach, in which investors bear part of the risk inherent in uncertain undertakings through their investment in nonbank entities.[27] However, there are several problems with the narrow banking model. Economies of scale would be lost; banks have dominated financial markets for many centuries, notwithstanding recent changes in OECD countries. This is in part because, as Calomiris and Kahn note, substantial information and enforcement capability are required for arm's-length, nonbank finance.[28] In addition, requiring banks to hold safer assets lowers the returns they will pay and would probably result in a shift of funds to the presumably less regulated, nonbank financial sector. These institutions, which would then dwarf their already large counterparts today, would truly be too big to fail. And if U.S. authorities could not allow the Chrysler Motor Corporation to fail, it is difficult to believe that many governments would permit a huge nonbank financial firm to fail.

With either narrow banking or increased liability limits in banking, the danger is therefore that government guarantees will migrate along with depositor funds to nonbanks. With more financial wealth in nonbanks, governments will be pressed to provide some guarantees on these funds. However, if governments can adhere to the principle of insuring only those deposits in narrow banks, the prospect of nonbanks growing in importance might be appealing.

A fourth option for authorities is to attempt to limit entry into banking sufficiently to increase the franchise value of bank licenses.[29] This proposal emerges from the U.S. experience of rising bank risk during the 1960s, as profits eroded as a result of the gradual increase in competition from nonbanks and foreign institutions.[30] Limiting entry will increase profits, the discounted value of which represents the franchise value of possessing a charter to do business as a bank. If this value is substantial, bank owners will try to ensure that they will be open and able to earn those profits; in other words, they will be motivated to behave in a safe manner. Bank licenses could either be given away or sold, though charging too high a price would reduce the franchise value and potentially lead to unsafe banking.

Few countries have completely open entry into banking, and most require that applicants have some initial capital, evidence of banking skills, and a reputation for honesty before granting a license. Some countries have insufficient competition because of various disincentives, from the small size of the potential market (such as those of a number of African economies) to confiscatory taxes on financial intermediation.[31] But giving away "admission tickets" into banking might reward corruption, because bribing officials in charge of licenses can be expected where licenses are valuable. Charging a high entry fee (initial capital) instead rewards previous beneficiaries of "the system," but it could allow new entrepreneurs to enter into banking, which proved to be a distinct advantage in early U.S. history.

The chief drawback of trying to raise franchise value is the difficulty in maintaining a lid on entry if profits are high. Authorities that attempt to establish excessive monopoly power by awarding relatively few charters would see the rise of nonbanks that perform many of the same functions. Relatedly, it is difficult to define the number of charters to grant, and some arbitrariness as to who receives them is unavoidable. Still, systems based on minimum capital ratios may have arbitrary requirements for capital, which could prompt disintermediation if the requirements are set too high. Although raising capital can drive intermediation efforts offshore, restricted entry could lead to an excess demand for bank licenses.[32] The best approach would call for balancing incentives for prudent banking and those encouraging competitive practices. Perhaps the most important feature of this new approach to financial regulation is that it would focus on the incentives facing bank owners. If these incentives are not structured to achieve both prudence and competition, bankers will naturally respond by taking on riskier exposures.

Finally, improved bank entry might be sought as the complete opposite of monopoly banking—namely, the free banking model in which anyone can establish a bank, with virtually no limits on that bank's activities. It should be clear that deposit insurance and free entry are incompatible; in concert with free entry, deposit insurance would attract undesirable applicants into the industry and encourage risk taking behavior. As in the United States and Scotland during their free banking eras, no deposit insurance should be provided. Even in the absence of deposit insurance, however, authorities would probably be unwise to permit totally free entry into banking.

Perhaps the key advantage of free banking is that it would scale back the supervisory apparatus that, in varying degrees, is part of each of the other systems. By requiring depositors to monitor banks in the absence of full or partial insurance, free banking enjoys the same advantages noted in the discussion of option one above (but also suffers from the same drawbacks). If liability limits remain too low, failures could result, with attendant pressure for government bailouts. Free banking appeared to work quite well in Scotland, but with unlimited liability. However, this was just one experiment. If liability limits were set too high, the provision of loans for risky undertakings might be in short supply.[33]

Whichever broad option is pursued, authorities should keep in mind that the bank failures are most commonly caused by insufficient diversification, albeit for various reasons.[34] Although the different options listed here should motivate owners to avoid concentration of risk, authorities should assist them by making sure that their regulations do not mandate or reward excessive portfolio concentration. In small economies, limits on capital flows do precisely this: if banks cannot invest abroad, their portfolios will necessarily be exposed to shocks in the markets for their leading export goods. Many prices will be affected when the terms of trade decline; the smaller the economy, the more true this will be. Authorities in small economies should therefore move aggressively to lift portfolio limits on banks. Indeed, a requirement that domestic banks in a small economy invest some portion of their assets abroad is not inconceivable. To ensure that these funds are not squandered on risky foreign investments, such investments could be limited to shares in diversified mutual funds, at least until the bankers have greater risk management expertise.

CONCLUSIONS, WITH GUIDELINES FOR SAFER BANKING

"The" right regulatory model for developing and transitional economies (and industrial countries as well) is not yet known, and it may well be unique to a country's institutional structure. Different institutions—the rules, laws, and customs that regulate economic activities— may be suited for and fit in better with certain kinds of banking and financial systems. However, the direction of reform is clear and has wide applicability. Aligning incentives for bank owners and managers to promote prudent risk taking would lift the excessive burden placed on bank supervisors to guarantee safe banking. If owners have more at stake in terms of their reputation, deposits, personal assets, or future expected profits, they can be expected to take greater measures to safeguard their bank. This is in sharp contrast to the present systems in most countries, with their limited liability, modest capital requirements, and some form of deposit guarantee.

One drawback of all of the proposals that have been discussed here is that they may tend to widen interest rate spreads either through less competition, higher capital requirements, or greater segmentation, or more generally by reducing government subsidies for risk taking. However, in the narrow banking or free banking variants, savers would likely face a variety of choices as to how much risk they need face. With any of these proposals, governments that have been restricting capital mobility have the option of increasing the ability of banks to diversify and thereby lower spreads, or to let in more foreign banks. Conversely, the less the ability to diversify risk, the higher will be the required capital or the expected future profits needed to ensure safe banking.

By widening spreads and by diverting local savings from domestic investment, these proposals appear to run counter to many current development efforts. However, by better protecting savers (and taxpayers!) and also by improving the local investment climate, authorities might be able to allow for greater diversification and to increase the supply of investable resources to the local economy. Most important, given the increasing evidence of the significance regarding efficiency of fund investment rather than simply the total level of savings, the proposals to better align bankers' incentives with prudent risk taking should help to enhance development through improved resource allocation. Even tiny improvements in factor productivity can pay substantial dividends, the benefits of regulatory reform will be well worth the cost.

REFERENCES

Akerlof, George A., and David M. Romer. 1993. "Looting: The Economic Underworld of Bankruptcy for Profit." *Brookings Papers on Economic Activity* 2: 1–60.

Bernanke, Ben. 1983. "Nonmonetary Effects of the Financial Crisis in the Propagation of the Great Depression." *American Economic Review* 73 (June): 257–76.

Boyd, John H., and Arthur J. Rolnick. 1989. "A Case for Reforming Federal Deposit Insurance." *Federal Reserve Bank of Minneapolis, 1988 Annual Report,* 3–15.

Calomiris, Charles W., and Charles M. Kahn. 1991. "The Role of Demandable Debt in Structuring Optimal Banking Arrangements." *American Economic Review* 81 (3): 497–513.

Calomiris, Charles W., and Eugene N. White. 1993. "The Origins of Federal Deposit Insurance." Paper presented at the NBER conference on the Political Economy of Regulation, May 20.

Caprio, Gerard, Jr., and others. 1994. *Financial Reform: Theory and Experience.* Cambridge University Press.

Caprio, Gerard, Jr., and Ross Levine. 1994. "Reforming Finance in Transitional Socialist Economies." *World Bank Research Observer* 9 (1): 1–24.

Caprio, Gerard, Jr., and Lawrence H. Summers. 1996. "Financial Reform: Beyond Laissez Faire." In *Stability in the Financial System,* edited by Dmitri B. Papadimitriou, pp. 400–421. Macmillan.

Chamley, Christophe, and Patrick Honohan. 1990. "Taxation of Financial Intermediation: Measurement Principles and Application to Five African Countries." Policy Research Working Paper 421. Washington: World Bank.

de Juan, Aristobulo. 1988. "From Good Bankers to Bad Bankers: Ineffective Supervision and Management Deterioration as Major Elements in Banking Crises." Washington: World Bank, Financial Policy and Systems Division.

Gertler, Mark, and Andrew Rose. 1994. "Finance, Public Policy, and Growth." In *Financial Reform: Theory and Experience,* edited by Gerard Caprio and others, 13–47. Cambridge University Press.

Keeley, Michael C. 1990. "Deposit Insurance, Risk, and Market Power in Banking." *American Economic Review* 80 (5): 1183–1200.

Litan, Robert E. 1987. *What Banks Should Do.* Brookings.

McKinnon, Ronald. 1973. *Money and Capital in Economic Development.* Brookings.

Rolnick, Arthur J. 1994. "Market Discipline as a Regulator of Bank Risk." In *Safeguarding the Banking System in an Environment of Financial Cycles,* edited by Richard E. Randall, 96–110. Federal Reserve Bank of Boston.

Schiantarelli, Fabio Izak Atiyas, Gerard Caprio, and John Harris. 1994. "Credit Where It Is Due? A Summary of Empirical Evidence." In *Financial Reform: Theory and Experience,* edited by Gerard Caprio and others, 64–81. Cambridge University Press.

Simons, Henry C. 1948. *Economic Policy for a Free Society.* University of Chicago Press.

Simons, Katerina, and Stephen Cross. 1991. "Do Capital Markets Predict Problems in Large Commercial Banks?" *New England Economic Review* (May/June): 51–56.

NOTES

1. McKinnon (1973).
2. Caprio and others (1994).
3. de Juan (1988).
4. Schiantarelli, Caprio, and Harris (1994).
5. Gertler and Rose (1994).

6. Caprio and others (1994). As I suggested previously, conclusions should be based, where possible, on the ability of intermediaries to raise funds and to allocate them prudently.

7. Information capital is the accumulation of information on clients and risks that banks build up over time. As Levine and I argued in Caprio and Levine (1994, chapter 3), banks will invest in information capital up to the point at which its marginal product equals the cost of additional information. The latter in general will be higher in developing countries, because of the shortage of accounting and auditing skills and standards, rating agencies, and the like. Also, prolonged financial repression often leads banks to underinvest in information capital, and to acquire it in uneconomic—and often highly protected—sectors.

8. Caprio and others (1994).

9. Bernanke (1983) associates the contraction of lending in the United States during the Great Depression with the destruction of information capital that was possessed by the several thousand failed banks.

10. Occasionally, government officials will point to French state-owned banks as evidence that state ownership can work in this industry. However, the losses experienced by Crédit Lyonnais, estimated at more than $10 billion, should put this example to rest. Also, the French state-owned banks performed as well as they did partly because of the government's unwillingness to interfere much in compensation decisions. Most governments hold wages in state banks to civil service levels, often a mere fraction of what private banks might pay.

11. In Caprio and Summers (1996) we argue that the increase in competition from nonbanks and foreign banks reduced the franchise value of bank licenses to the point that bank owners became less concerned with safe-and-sound banking. If interstate branching restrictions had been lifted in the 1950s, the resulting consolidation of U.S. banking might have left the industry with only 2,000 large, diversified, and highly profitable banks, whose owners would have had a greater stake in ensuring that they would be around to collect these large profits.

12. New Zealand authorities have been moving away from supervising the financial system, based on the argument that supervision creates a public expectation that the authorities are guaranteeing a return on their funds. However, it is too early to tell if this system will be able to ward off instability, or to persevere in the face of it.

13. Rolnick (1994).

14. Even with high rewards for prudent risk taking, and notwithstanding good screening by the authorities in charge of granting licenses, there will

always be some bankers with a sufficiently high rate of time preference that they will be motivated to "loot." See Akerlof and Romer (1993).

15. Because private banks can afford to buy the very best "rocket scientists" (the Wall Street term for the mathematicians, physicists, and computer scientists who work on inventing new, often option-based financial products), the odds are that supervisory agencies may not be able to uncover soon enough the excessive risks associated with these products.

16. Indeed, what first attracted supervisors' attention was its rapid growth rate and high real interest rates (which eventually reached 30 percent to 50 percent).

17. See *Global Finance*, September 1994.

18. See Simons and Cross (1991), who note that not only does the U.S. stock market fail to predict bank performance, but in the case of downgrading by supervisors, insiders also bought stock more often than not in the immediate preceding quarter.

19. Caprio and Summers (1996).

20. Calomiris and White (1993).

21. Boyd and Rolnick (1989).

22. In assessing bank soundness, supervisors look at the so-called CAMEL variables—capital, asset quality, management, earnings, and liquidity. Even modest capital holdings will suffice if the other variables are strong.

23. Speculation about the consequences of applying the death penalty or various forms of torture are beyond the scope of my discussion, however much they might intrigue enraged authorities and taxpayers who have paid for the shenanigans of "ebullient" bankers.

24. This solution used to be recommended for pollution, as it is difficult to estimate the benefits and costs of raising pollution abatement taxes. This has led some practical economists to recommend that, rather than to just do nothing, governments should raise taxes to see if the resulting level of pollution is desirable, given the costs. Unsafe banking can be treated as a similar, unsavory externality.

25. Calomiris and White (1993).

26. Simons (1948); Litan (1987).

27. In theory, Islamic banking, in which neither deposits nor "loans" bear fixed interest, was to be a system in which banks behave like mutual funds. However, perhaps because of the demand by lenders and users of funds for some certainty, these banks usually provide some guaranteed minimum return on deposits and also put limits on the fluctuation of the return on investment.

28. Calomiris and Kahn (1991).

29. Caprio and Summers (1996).

30. Keeley (1990).

31. Chamley and Honohan (1990).

32. Although a more monopolistic banking system would be characterized by higher spreads, bankers presumably would figure out that they need to be more competitive on the liability side, as depositors can be expected to be more mobile than borrowers.

33. To be sure, there may be a trade-off between society's preferences for venture finance and safe-and-sound banking.

34. Bankers may concentrate their risks for various reasons: limited choice, assets whose prices move in a highly correlated fashion, linked ownership—concentrating loans on a firm that owns the bank, or one run by the bank president's relative—or more generally an inability to plan. See de Juan (1988).

Chapter 10

CLAUDIO GONZALEZ-VEGA

Nonbank Institutions in Financial Sector Reform

In this chapter I discuss the role of nonbank financial institutions in financial development and reform and the implications of nonbank financial activity for the speed and sequencing of reforms. My analysis distinguishes among three types of nonbank organizations: the upward-looking innovations, the downward-looking innovations, and those organizations that result from regulatory avoidance. The two types of innovations represent solutions to difficult information, risk, and incentive problems that are not easily resolved by traditional banks. Avoidance, in turn, results from lack of competitive neutrality of the regulatory framework. As with banks, for stability nonbank organizations require prudential regulation and supervision that protects competitive neutrality while avoiding financial repression.

Much of the literature on financial reform has focused on macroeconomic policy management, efficiency of the payments system, deregulation and privatization of financial and nonfinancial enterprises, and development of capital markets. Particular attention has been paid to the regulation and supervision of banks. This emphasis is quite appropriate; in a repressive policy framework or unstable macroeconomic environment, few formal financial institutions can flourish. Macroeconomic stability, low rates of inflation and, in particular, fiscal control are prerequisites for successful financial reform.[1] Increased efficiency of the payments system is also critical, as a tool to reduce transaction costs and foster market integration. Banks are important precisely because their performance is closely linked to the efficiency of the payments system. Moreover, because monetary assets (the liabilities of the banking system) dominate the financial portfolios of savers in developing economies, banks represent the most important external source of funding of investment. Banks thus matter because of their key role in providing both monetization and intermediation services to the economy. The emergence of strong, stable banks is critical to economic progress in countries in transition from a command economy to a market allocation of resources.[2]

The prudential regulation and supervision of banks matters, in turn, because of the potential negative externalities associated with bank failures.[3] In the absence of regulation, bank instability may be higher than is socially desirable. Also, the volume of deposits may decline, in light of the potentially opportunistic behavior of bank managers and owners at the expense of depositors. Such market imperfections, combined with the breakdown of feasible collective remedial action by depositors, provide the rationale for state regulation and supervision of banks and other deposit-taking institutions.[4]

THREE TYPES OF NONBANK FINANCIAL INSTITUTIONS

Although the emphasis placed on banks is understandable, in this chapter I focus on nonbank financial institutions. What role should they play in financial reform and institutional development? What are the implications of nonbank operations for the sequencing of reforms and institutional development efforts?

As income grows and the economy becomes more diversified, the first category—the upward-looking innovations—leads to a more sophisticated financial system, catering to the complex demands of large commercial firms and wealthy investors. Downward-looking innovations, instead, bring into the formal system clienteles previously left out of the supply of basic financial services, thus expanding the frontier of the system.[5] Finally, market participants subject to repressive regulation discover new, unregulated financial activities that become competitive through regulatory avoidance.[6]

Upward-Looking Innovations

As Levine described in chapter 2 of this book, there are predictable patterns of development for financial market structures.[7] As income levels increase, the size of the domestic market grows, the country's institutional infrastructure develops, and more complex contracts emerge. In addition, new, specialized nonbank intermediaries such as mutual funds, pension funds, insurance companies, investment banks, venture capital funds, and the like respond to demand for a wider set of risk-return combinations. With the emergence of these new entities, the structure of the financial system becomes increasingly complex and diversified.

Although these nonbank financial organizations play increasingly important roles in the economy, they rely on an advanced degree of organizational development and can only operate if the appropriate legal structures, institutional mechanisms, and information processes are available. For this reason, they are usually anticipated in a future stage rather than the present one of financial policy reform and institutional development in the low-income developing countries or economies in transition.[8] Nonetheless, the authorities must anticipate the emergence of these nonbank financial institutions and must develop the organizational infrastructure essential for their efficient operation. In particular, there is a need for a regulatory framework to reduce instability and for contract enforcement mechanisms to prevent fraud and default. However, these measures could come at a later stage in processes of institution building. They would not be a priority for foreign assistance; in the short run, developing countries and economies in transition should be encouraged to focus mostly on building better banks.

Regulatory Avoidance

A second set of nonbank financial institutions results from regulatory avoidance in the face of repressive policies and constraints on financial intermediary operations. Financial repression encompasses all forms of regulation that distort and reduce the efficiency of financial markets.[9] Typically, these regulations seek to tax or subsidize financial transactions or otherwise to influence resource allocation by setting constraints on financial transactions. Repressive interventions include credit subsidies, mandatory credit allocations and targeted loans, confiscatory reserve requirements, inflation and overvaluation of the domestic currency, and excessive restrictions to entry into the market. Efforts to avoid these regulations may take the form of new products and services or new types of financial intermediaries.[10]

Regulatory avoidance is particularly likely when regulation is partial or nonneutral. The competitive neutrality of any regulatory framework is necessary to provide a level playing field for all market participants. This allows for development of institutional comparative advantages and minimizes the regulatory avoidance triggered by any discriminatory treatment. In the case of repressive and nonneutral regulatory frameworks, avoidance may have several adverse consequences. For example, otherwise law-abiding regulated institutions may undertake risky, nonregulated activities. If reserve requirements on deposits are excessive, banks may design new quasi-deposit instruments not subject to such requirements (for example, *fideicomisos*, or funds in trust), thus undermining the original intent of the regulator. In other cases, given constraints on loan transactions, nonregulated activities may lead to the accumulation of off–balance sheet and other contingent liabilities.[11] This behavior will increase risk in the system and complicate the enforcement of capital adequacy requirements. In Ecuador in the early 1980s, for example, constraints on interest rates and excessive reserve requirements repressed domestic funds mobilization and led domestic banks to guarantee loans by foreign banks rather than to lend money themselves. After a major devaluation, when they and their clienteles were not able to face the accompanying foreign exchange risk, a massive bailout by the Central Bank was necessary, with substantial quasi-fiscal costs.[12]

Recently, prudential regulation in Latin America has attempted to follow the norms of the Basel Convention. These norms include capital adequacy requirements computed on the sum of the weighted risk amount of assets and off–balance sheet contingency accounts, multiplied by a capital adequacy factor. If banks are reluctant to increase their capital base, they will attempt to maintain few of the assets (such as loans) subject to the highest risk weights. Moreover, to avoid increased capital contributions, banks may adopt policies that unintendedly increase their risk, but the authorities cannot easily recognize what is happening.

The challenge for the prudential regulator is to design risk weights that lead to appropriate capital requirements without inducing unanticipated risk taking. This purpose is not always achieved. Gómez

has shown that when Ecuador adopted a 3 percent capital requirement on the current loan portfolio, a 5 percent requirement on the
off–balance sheet contingency accounts, and a 100 percent requirement on accrued interest, it became more attractive for banks to provide clients with a guarantee on a loan from a third party than to grant
a direct loan.[13] This inclination was accentuated by high reserve requirements on domestic deposits. As a result, the four largest banks of
Ecuador had off–balance sheet contingency accounts of between 102
and 310 percent of their loan portfolio. These loan guarantees are
high-risk contingent liabilities when denominated in foreign currency,
as they were in Ecuador, if the bank moves to disburse the funds
immediately to honor the guarantee and then suffers a foreign-
exchange loss. Eventually, a major devaluation put the Ecuadoran
banks in the position of being unable to honor these loan guarantees.

So as to locate some of their activities beyond the jurisdiction of the
local regulatory framework, regulatory avoidance can also lead to the
establishment of offshore operations by domestic financial intermediaries. In the case of Costa Rica, for example, it has been estimated
that off–balance sheet liabilities that substitute for regular deposits
account for 15 percent of the banks' productive assets, but their offshore operations approximate the size of their domestic operations.[14]
Regulation at these offshore sites is less constraining. The mixing of
domestic-regulated and offshore-unregulated operations thus mas-
sively complicates the task of bank supervision. For example, the
information contained in the financial statements of the domestic
banks does not always provide a full picture of their risk exposure; the
banks arbitrarily add, omit, or mix records from one to the other
operation. Frequently, they attempt to charge most of their combined
fixed costs to the operations of the domestic headquarters, but accrue
most earnings at the offshore subsidiary. In these circumstances, financial ratios and other indicators mean little for prudential supervision. Costa Rica is not alone among countries saddled by financial
repression in having banks find ways to relocate the site of their
operations offshore in attempts to avoid the losses resulting from the
implicit taxes.

Furthermore, initiatives for regulatory avoidance may lead to the
establishment of nonregulated parallel domestic financial markets. In
the mid-1980s, for example, close to 1,000 unregulated *financieras* and

other nonbank intermediaries operated side by side with more than two dozen regulated banks in Santo Domingo, capital of the Dominican Republic. Often the unregulated entities were subsidiaries of the regulated banks.[15] This was a dramatic example of the exit effects associated with excessive bank regulation. Because of this exit, repeated attempts to regulate the financial sector (each new effort more strict than the time before) progressively resulted in a shrinking regulated segment of the market and in less overall control by the banking authorities.

However, the emergence of these unregulated parallel markets helped to alleviate the negative consequences of financial repression. Deposits were kept in Santo Domingo that would have otherwise migrated to New York as flight capital and loans were supplied to marginal clienteles displaced from the shrinking portfolios of regulated banks. Nevertheless, depositors as well as intermediaries in these nonregulated markets demanded higher risk premiums. These premiums, along with high transaction costs for depositors and for borrowers, increased the total cost of borrowed funds. The parallel markets did not therefore look like the efficient curb markets of the neostructuralist world.[16] With high real rates of interest and missing prudential supervision, adverse selection effects and portfolio risks increased and opportunistic behavior flourished. Eventually, some *financiera* owners fled under cover of night, causing a domino effect that led to a collapse of the parallel market and even to failure of some regulated banks with close links to nonregulated intermediaries.

Transitional countries face a dilemma in attempting to steer a course between the ill effects of too much and too little regulation. Even if a theoretical rationale exists for intervention, the universally observed negative consequences from financial repression suggest that inappropriate regulation may frequently be more dangerous than no regulation at all.[17] What really matters are the actual effects and not the stated objectives of regulation. Too often good intentions of poorly designed regulations are outweighed by the unintended evils.[18] Moreover, highly effective supervision efforts are sometimes the worst of all, if they are directed at making sure that repressive restrictions are strictly enforced. Indeed, the potential damage is greatest when repressive regulation is so successful that it prevents all regulatory avoidance.[19] Therefore, the solution is not to enforce bad rules more effectively but to eliminate the original financial repression. Failing that, regulatory avoidance would be the lesser evil than strict compliance with the repressive mandates.

The best solution is for countries to adopt prudential (as distinct from repressive) regulation to promote the stability, efficiency, and soundness of the banking system.[20] Prudential efforts attempt to protect small depositors against fraud or failure. When prudential regulation is nondistorting, it relies on mandates of a general nature that induce all market participants to adhere to standard rules that protect the stability of the system, mostly through compatible incentives. In developing countries and economies in transition, as repressive financial regulation is dismantled and prudential supervision adopted, the authorities must strive to achieve *competitive neutrality*—that is, instruments and financial organizations that are essentially the same must receive equal treatment. The regulatory environment must provide all market players with a level playing field early on.[21] If particular intermediaries are granted artificial advantages because of charter names, ownership structure, or client orientation, allocative efficiency will be reduced and regulatory avoidance encouraged.[22]

Because frequent innovations and regulatory avoidance are inevitable, the regulatory framework should respond quickly to changes in financial products and market structure. Technological change spreads rapidly in financial markets, as both product and process innovations are easily replicated by competitors. Prudential regulators must keep up with these changes, pushing their authority beyond banks to include nonbank entities and adapting their powers to the new pressures on the supervisory agency.[23] However, regulators tend to react more slowly than the organizations that they supervise. In this regulatory dialectic (regulation, avoidance, reregulation), therefore, the authorities tend to lag behind and to be slow in recognizing the true importance of emerging forms of yet-to-be-regulated risk.[24] In this context, a simplistic concept of reform sequencing is particularly inappropriate. Effective prudential regulation and supervision is a continuing process, moving with the evolution of market forces, technological innovation, and changes in organizational structures. Institutional development is not about "this first and that next," but about the evolution of a broad-based set of interrelated components.

Downward-Looking Innovations

Some of the most interesting and challenging issues of financial sector development concern the downward-looking innovations in the provision of financial services—that is, services to households and firms not usually considered creditworthy by formal financial institutions. Rather than creating increasingly sophisticated arrangements in the most advanced market segments, innovations in this case enlarge financial markets by serving new market niches and by responding to basic demands by clienteles not yet reached by institutional finance. This task, though perhaps less glamorous than the development of capital markets or financial derivatives, is nevertheless important and equally challenging for developing countries and economies in transition. Foreign assistance should concentrate in this area.

Initiatives to expand the frontier of financial markets come from two sources. The first is from entrepreneurial intermediaries and investors who attempt to bring formal financial services to clienteles who have not used them before. Their innovations improve risk management and reduce transaction costs, creating opportunities for profitable financial intermediation in new market niches. These innovators may include exceptional bankers who are willing to reach downward into new market segments, or emerging nonbank organizations that can generate comparative advantages in supplying financial services to difficult clienteles. In the second case, initiatives may also come from government and donor intervention, either directly by providing financial services to specific target groups through state-owned banks or nongovernment organizations, or indirectly by requiring existing financial intermediaries to lend to those clienteles. Government actions may also promote this class of nonbank institutions by improving the physical and institutional infrastructure for reaching new clienteles, promoting research and development in financial technologies, or capitalizing organizations ready to accept the challenge of dealing with households and small businesses previously without access to these financial services.[25]

The complexities of serving new groups is apparent from the history of targeted financial market interventions. The prevalence of failed attempts at influencing the prices and quantities of financial transactions by decree on behalf of poor people suggests that it is desirable to work with, rather than against, financial market forces.[26] In the 1950s, particularly in rural areas of developing countries, the finance problem was defined as a generalized lack of access to formal, institutional credit, coupled with rates of interest that were too high and dispersed for short-term informal credit transactions. At that time, these problems were diagnosed mostly as a reflection of two types of market failure: Commercial banks were seen as too conservative, and moneylenders were thought to enjoy excessive monopoly power.[27] In most developing countries, the typical policy answers to these "problems" and to the "failure" of markets to provide financial services to politically preferred clienteles were the creation of government-owned specialized development banks and the establishment of subsidized, targeted credit programs. These interventions were prevalent among strategies of financial repression considered deplorable by the standards of contemporary financial reforms, and they are cited as striking manifestations of the shortcomings of government intervention in financial markets.[28]

Economic theory, however, has once again called attention to market failure, in the form of asymmetric information and opportunistic behavior leading to moral hazard and adverse selection.[29] Nevertheless, such theoretical efforts do not lead to robust recommendations for government intervention, nor do they suggest feasible instruments for such intervention.[30] Now that the high costs of government failure and of the rent-seeking and unproductive activities that accompany protectionist interventions are much better understood, we should be extremely cautious in embracing new forms of government intervention to reach marginal clienteles.[31]

The problems of rural financial markets also reflected, moreover, the high transaction costs of an inadequate physical and institutional infrastructure, including inappropriate definitions of property rights and absence of effective mechanisms for contract design and enforcement.[32] Development of the required infrastructure may still be a critical function for the state. But the form that such intervention might take should be in the provision of public goods rather than in interfering with the pricing of services or in directly allocating credit. This line of thought implies a different view of the state's role in processes of economic development.

THE FINANCE PROBLEM IN DEVELOPING COUNTRIES

What should be the new role for the state in finance and economic growth, broadly defined? To answer this question, a more productive approach would be to better understand the fundamental nature of the problem of access to finance in developing countries. In these nations there are some economic agents with wealth but without attractive investment opportunities of their own. There are also large numbers of agents with unexploited opportunities but lacking sufficient funds to take full advantage of these opportunities. The challenge of financial intermediation is to match those "with money but no projects" to those "with projects but no money." This matching is not easy.

Problems emerge because potential borrowers may be unable or unwilling to repay loans. As a result, any lender's supply of credit to a particular borrower depends on having adequate information about the borrower's reliability and about the nature of the productive opportunity being financed. In the absence of sufficient information, the loan will not be granted because of the high degree of uncertainty about repayment. In addition, because of asymmetric information, opportunities for moral hazard emerge. For example, individuals who have already borrowed may slacken in their efforts to make the project successful or may change the nature of the project, making it riskier. Because of fears that this may happen, lenders need to monitor borrower behavior closely. If monitoring is too costly, lenders either restrict the amount of the loan or do not lend at all. Furthermore, if higher interest rates attract riskier borrowers, adverse selection problems may arise and may induce lenders to engage in credit rationing.[33] The financial market also requires a framework for a cost-effective legal enforcement of contracts. In the absence of the required institutional infrastructure, the costs of enforcement may be too high for potential lenders, and potential borrowers would not otherwise have access to formal loans.

When these difficulties are significant, economic agents may be constrained in their access to capital and excluded from investing and undertaking profitable projects. A traditional solution to this problem is to use collateral: the pledge of comparatively liquid assets about which there is adequate knowledge, or mechanisms for foreclosure and cost-effective contract enforcement.[34] In collateral-based lending, the liquidation value of the assets is typically less than their value if in continued use by the borrower; thus, the amount of investment that can be undertaken may be constrained. This type of lending relies on the availability of collateralizable assets within a well-defined structure of property rights and with cost-effective institutions for contract enforcement. It also implies that there are markets where the value of such assets can be established. Few of these preconditions are present for marginal clienteles in developing or transition economies.

The alternative is information-based lending, by individuals who possess information about the borrower or his or her line of business and who can monitor the borrower at low costs. Informal financial markets rely on these information-intensive lending technologies. Pervasive informal financial arrangements have been partially successful in overcoming information, incentive, and enforcement problems and in supplying a range of specific financial services to poor people in developing and transitional countries. Repayment-relevant information and opportunities for monitoring are obtained by local informal lenders at low marginal cost through their daily interactions with potential borrowers. Noninstitutional mechanisms for contract enforcement, mostly based on the value of reputation in personalized market settings, facilitate informal financial transactions. However, informal financial arrangements suffer from a number of limitations. These shortcomings are the reverse side of their virtues: informal markets are grounded in the community and as a result are limited by the wealth constraints and the covariant risks of the local economy. Their frontier is narrow geographically and their time horizon is short. In sum, informal arrangements provide only some financial services, in small amounts, for short periods of time. They are therefore not good vehicles for long-term investment. More important, because they are cost effective only in the immediate neighborhood, they do not overcome market segmentation and contribute little to the most important function of finance: the integration of markets. For this critical task, formal finance with a national scope is required.[35]

The key to reaching marginal clientele is to design public or private institutions geared to the size of the market and compatible with the nature of the clientele.[36] Most of the time traditional banking, for example, is prohibitively expensive for dealing with poor clients. Both lender and borrower transaction costs are too high. But traditional banks can adopt strategies to reach new clients.[37] Such efforts may include the restructuring of public development banks, to expand the scope of their operations.[38] Nonbank organizations possess, for their part, comparative advantages in information and enforcement of contracts among poor people and other nontraditional clienteles. They may be eventually upgraded to become banks or to mimic them, and in general to acquire some of the advantages of greater formality. In such a case, they will be covered by the formal financial regulatory framework. The process of institutional experimentation may also eventually lead to creation of entirely new types of financial institutions.

In many cases of successful institutional development, it appears important to add a deposit mobilization dimension to the services supplied. This is because of the intrinsic value of deposit services for the clientele and for the economy as a whole, and also because deposit mobilization brings financial discipline to the intermediary. Deposit mobilization offers valuable services to savers (who typically have a high demand for depositing facilities) and contributes to the viability of the financial institutions.

APPROPRIATE REGULATION AND SUPERVISION FOR DIFFERENT FINANCIAL INSTITUTIONS

Deposit taking introduces threats to the stability of the financial system and raises issues of depositor protection that must be resolved before this important financial service is encouraged. Prudential regulation and supervision are indispensable in the case of intermediaries that take deposits, to protect small savers from the opportunistic behavior or incompetence of management and for the system's stability.[39] Public or donor funds may also help capitalize nonbank financial organizations, through grant-equity or quasi-equity contributions, shareholder participation in new intermediaries, or the recapitalization of government-owned banks. Internal control tools are critical when the public sector is a shareholder in a financial intermediary.

Shareholders need the means to exercise performance monitoring and the incentives to do so effectively. An understanding of the threats faced by the organization as well as the design of appropriate incentives for managers and board members are both necessary. Accountability of public servants in government-owned agencies is particularly relevant, as is the monitoring of public sector funds granted as equity or quasi-equity contributions to private and nongovernment financial organizations.

Requirements for safe deposit taking as well as adequate vigilance of public sector funds will normally call for some form of government regulation and supervision. During the past decade there has been considerable progress in the development of new organizations for the prudential regulation and supervision of banks.[40] The developed nations have adopted Basel Convention standards, and several developing countries have adapted them to their particular circumstances. Strong superintendencies of banks have been created in many developing countries (Chile, Bolivia, Ecuador, Costa Rica, the Dominican Republic, and Indonesia, among others). But building such institutions is a long-term and difficult process for most nations. In practice, many new superintendencies encounter serious problems in implementing prudential rules. They are also frequently overburdened by their new responsibilities and have only limited resources to complete their more demanding tasks. These complications militate against lending to and mobilizing the deposits of poor clients. In instances of reorienting lending practices to include poor people, some bank superintendencies have found it difficult to adjust their prudential criteria to cover loan portfolios not based on traditional collateral requirements. In implementing risk-weighted capital requirements, for example, they have tended to penalize loans not guaranteed by traditional collateral or based on audited financial statements. Prudential standards must be revised to make them friendlier toward lending to poor clients and still offer appropriate protection to depositors and to the stability of the financial system.

There are some indications that bank supervisors are learning to examine and evaluate portfolios based on character lending and on the close monitoring of borrowers, rather than on traditional collateral.[41] As nonbank intermediaries are upgraded and become institutions that take deposits, however, this poses additional risks and challenges for prudential regulators. Deposit mobilization requires the kind of regulation and supervision that can treat various bank and nonbank intermediaries differently. Idiosyncratic risks arise as a result of the institutional design of some nonbank intermediaries; some intermediary types, for example, have a diffused ownership structure. This design may cause their "owners" to not oversee operations closely enough and to provide inadequate internal control, thereby increasing the risks of failure. Bank superintendencies face problems as they strive to maintain a level playing field, as required by competitive neutrality, while being flexible enough to regulate these new nonbank institutions. Their examination tools have been appropriate for their traditional customers, the private commercial banks. These tools and methodologies are not easily adaptable to the peculiarities of such nonbank intermediaries as credit unions, village banks, and nongovernment organizations. Bank examiners need to design different early-warning indicators. The structure of assets and liabilities of the nonbank intermediary and the typical behavior of the clientele differ from traditional banking scenarios.

Microfinance intermediaries come in a large variety of institutional designs and legal charters and function in diverse economic and legal environments. The range of ownership varies—from financial intermediaries without specific owners, to private commercial banks that have found a market niche in serving poor people (such as BancoSol in Bolivia), to client-owned financial intermediaries (such as credit cooperatives and village banks), to state-owned banks (such as Bank Rakyat Indonesia). Nonprivate financial organizations with no clearly defined owners seldom have optimum levels of internal control. A lack of effective internal control increases the risk of illiquidity or insolvency prudential regulators must face.

Some traditional standards of prudential regulation, such as capital adequacy requirements and prohibition of related loans, may not even make sense when there are no owners or when the owners are clients (as in credit unions). The nature of the incentives resulting from each one of the institutional structures of nonbank intermediaries implies different behaviors in the presence of capital adequacy regulations. For nongovernment organizations, incentive-compatible regulations must be designed that go beyond simple capital adequacy requirements. However, these requirements are sufficient to elicit the desired behavior from commercial private banks. For credit cooperatives, which do have owners, the problem is that the owners pursue their own objectives and may not care if the organization fails to maximize its profits. Net borrowers, for example, may benefit even if reduced organizational profits come at the expense of net savers. These conflicts increase the risk that management will pursue its own interests and that the institution will prove unstable.[42]

The diversity of nonbank financial intermediaries is compounded by the range of the economic and legal environments in which they operate. Microentrepreneurs borrow in countries as dissimilar as the Gambia and Chile, where the infrastructure, legal systems, human capital, and the financial markets are extreme opposites. This diversity makes it impossible to provide a simple recipe for the regulation of these organizations. No general cost-benefit analysis is possible, for the relative scarcity of the inputs necessary for regulation (for example, trained bank examiners) changes the method of assessing costs and benefits of supervision from country to country.

The call for differentiated regulation is not incompatible with the principle of competitive neutrality called for here. Equality of treatment is not assured by treating unequals equally. Rather, the idea is to allow for a diversity of organizations compatible with the multiple needs of the market, while designing the regulatory framework to cope with the resulting variety.[43] Many nonbank institutions are comparatively new. As experience accumulates, a more solid and useful empirical body of knowledge will be created. Providing credit to small borrowers and depository services to small savers will become more attractive if countries can avoid the sudden policy backlashes that frequently result from the failure of improperly regulated intermediaries. Regulatory failures and policy backlashes alike jeopardize progress toward improving access small entrepreneurs might have to financial services.

REFERENCES

Adams, Dale W., Douglas H. Graham, and J. D. Von Pischke, eds. 1984. *Undermining Rural Development with Cheap Credit.* Boulder, Colo.: Westview Press.

Bencivenga, Valeria, and Bruce Smith. 1991. "Financial Intermediation and Endogenous Growth." *Review of Economic Studies* 58 (April): 195–209.

Benston, George J., and others. 1986. *Perspectives on Safe and Sound Banking: Past, Present, and Future.* MIT Press.

Besley, Timothy. 1994. "How Do Market Failures Justify Interventions in Rural Credit Markets?" *World Bank Research Observer* 9 (January): 27–48.

Camacho-Castro, Arnoldo, and Claudio Gonzalez-Vega. 1994. "Supervisión Bancaria en Centroamérica." In *Regulación, Competencia y Eficiencia en la Banca Costarricense*, edited by Claudio Gonzalez-Vega and Edna Camacho-Mejía. San José, Costa Rica: The Ohio State University and Academia de Centroamérica.

Camacho-Mejía, Edna, and Claudio Gonzalez-Vega. 1994. "Estructura, Regulación y Supervisión de la Banca." In *Regulación, Competencia y Eficiencia en la Banca Costarricense*, edited by Claudio Gonzalez-Vega and Edna Camacho-Mejía. San José, Costa Rica: The Ohio State University and Academia de Centroamérica.

Caprio, Gerard, and Ross Levine. 1994. "Reforming Finance in Transitional Socialist Economies." *World Bank Research Observer* 9 (January): 1–24.

Chaves, Rodrigo A., and Claudio Gonzalez-Vega. 1994. "Principles of Regulation and Prudential Supervision and Their Relevance for Microenterprise Finance Organizations." In *The New World of Microenterprise Finance: Building Healthy Financial Institutions for the Poor*, edited by Maria Otero and Elisabeth Rhyne. West Hartford, Conn.: Kumarian Press.

_____. 1996. "The Design of Successful Rural Financial Intermediaries: Evidence from Indonesia." *World Development* 24 (January): 65–78.

Dauhajre, Andrés. 1986. *Reforma Financiera en Pequeñas Economías Abiertas.* Santo Domingo, Dominican Republic: Centro de Estudios Monetarios y Bancarios.

Goldsmith, Raymond. 1969. *Financial Structure and Development.* Yale University Press.

Gómez, Gustavo. 1994. "Hidden Distortions in Banks' Capital Adequacy Requirements." Washington: Nathan Associates, Inc.

Gonzalez-Vega, Claudio. 1993. "From Policies, to Technologies, to Organizations: The Evolution of The Ohio State University Vision of Rural Financial Markets." Economics and Sociology Occasional Paper 2062. Columbus: The Ohio State University.

_____. 1994a. "La Reforma Financiera en Ecuador: Apuntes para una Evaluación." Quito: Instituto Centroamericano de Administración de Empresas (INCAE).

_____. 1994b. "Do Financial Institutions Have a Role in Assisting the Poor?" Economics and Sociology Occasional Paper No. 2169. Columbus: The Ohio State University.

_____. 1994c. "Stages in the Evolution of Thought on Rural Finance. A Vision from The Ohio State University." Economics and Sociology Occasional Paper No. 2134. Columbus: The Ohio State University.

Gonzalez-Vega, Claudio, and Douglas H. Graham. 1995. "State-owned Agricultural Development Banks: Lessons and Opportunities for Microfinance." Economics and Sociology Occasional Paper 2245. Columbus: The Ohio State University.

Gonzalez-Vega, Claudio, and Luis Mesalles-Jorba. 1993. "La Economía Política de la Nacionalización Bancaria: El Caso de Costa Rica." In *Reforma Financiera en Costa Rica: Perspectivas y Propuestas*, edited by Claudio Gonzalez-Vega and Thelmo Vargas-Madrigal. San José, Costa Rica: Academia de Centroamérica and The Ohio State University.

Gonzalez-Vega, Claudio, and James E. Zinser. 1987. "Regulated and Non-Regulated Financial and Foreign Exchange Markets and Income Inequality in the Dominican Republic." In *Economic Reform and Stabilization in Latin America*, edited by Michael H. Connolly and Claudio Gonzalez-Vega, 195–216. Praeger.

Holmstrom, Bengt. 1993. "Financing of Investment in Eastern Europe: A Theoretical Perspective." Working Paper Series 74. Washington: Institute for Policy Reform.

Kane, Edward. 1977. "Good Intentions and Unintended Evil: The Case against Selective Credit Allocation." *Journal of Money, Credit and Banking* 9 (February): 55–69.

_____. 1984. "Political Economy of Subsidizing Agricultural Credit in Developing Countries." In *Undermining Rural Development with Cheap Credit*, edited by Dale W. Adams, Douglas H. Graham, and J. D. Von Pischke, 166–82. Boulder, Colo.: Westview Press.

_____. 1985. *The Gathering Crisis in Federal Deposit Insurance*. MIT Press.

Kaufman, George G. 1988. "Bank Runs: Causes, Benefits, and Costs." *Cato Journal* 7 (Winter): 559–88.

King, R., and Ross Levine. 1993. "Finance and Growth: Schumpeter Might Be Right." *Quarterly Journal of Economics* 108 (August): 717–37.

Krahnen, Jan Pieter, and Reinhard H. Schmidt. 1994. *Development Finance as Institution Building: A New Approach to Poverty-Oriented Banking*. Boulder, Colo.: Westview Press.

McKinnon, Ronald I. 1973. *Money and Capital in Economic Development*. Brookings.

McKinnon, Ronald I. 1991. *The Order of Economic Liberalization: Financial Control in a Transition to a Market Economy*. Johns Hopkins University Press.

Myint, Hla. 1992. "Organizational Dualism and Economic Development." In *Development Economics*, edited by Deepak Lal. Brookfield, Vt.: Edward Elgar Publishing.

Poyo, Jeffrey, Claudio Gonzalez-Vega, and Nelson Aguilera-Alfred. 1993. "The Depositor as a Principal in Public Development Banks and Credit Unions: Illustrations from the Dominican Republic." Economics and Sociology Occasional Paper 2061. Columbus: The Ohio State University.

Rashid, Mansorra, and Robert Townsend. 1994. "Targeting Credit and Insurance: Efficiency, Mechanism Design, and Program Evaluation." ESP Discussion Paper Series. Washington: World Bank.

Shaw, Edward S. 1973. *Financial Deepening in Economic Development*. Oxford University Press.

Stiglitz, Joseph E. 1993. *Financial Systems for Eastern Europe's Emerging Democracies*. San Francisco: International Center for Economic Growth.

Stiglitz, Joseph E., and Andrew Weiss. 1981. "Credit Rationing in Markets with Imperfect Information." *American Economic Review* 4 (3): 393–410.

Trigo-Loubiere, Jacques. Forthcoming. "Regulation and Supervision of Microfinance Institutions: The Bolivian Experience." In *From Margin to Mainstream: The Regulation and Supervision of Microfinance Development*, edited by Maria Otero and Rachael Rock. Boston: ACCION International.

Vittas, Dimitri. 1992. *Financial Regulation: Changing the Rules of the Game*. Washington: World Bank.

Von Pischke, J. D. 1991. *Finance at the Frontier: Debt Capacity and the Role of Credit in the Private Economy*. Washington: World Bank.

NOTES

1. McKinnon (1991).

2. Caprio and Levine (1994).

3. Kaufman (1988).

4. Chaves and Gonzalez-Vega (1994).

5. Von Pischke (1991).

6. Kane (1977).

7. See also King and Levine (1993); Goldsmith (1969).

8. See Stiglitz (1993) for the development of equity markets.

9. Shaw (1973); McKinnon (1973).

10. Kane (1977). Gonzalez-Vega and Mesalles-Jorba (1993) discuss rent-seeking in this context.

11. Off–balance sheet activities categorize formal and informal commitments that generate contingent claims against a financial institution's resources. They are typically agreements to provide or to guarantee credit and to

deliver various other customer services on a standby basis. Because these agreements are offered contingently, generally accepted accounting principles do not require associated claims to be valued and entered on balance sheets of the contracting parties. Although accountants have designated the associated claims as off–balance sheet items, economic analysis must consider them coequal elements of an institution's generalized or market-value balance sheet (Kane [1985]). Thus, although off–balance sheet liabilities may not currently affect the intermediary's balance sheet, they generate a claim on its assets in the near future. Thus they represent actual contractual obligations that imply risks and that might trigger insolvency overnight.

12. Gonzalez-Vega (1994a).

13. Gómez (1994). Part of the reason is that this requirement is sensitive to nominal interest rates, which rise with inflation.

14. Camacho-Mejía and Gonzalez-Vega (1994).

15. Gonzalez-Vega and Zinser (1987).

16. Dauhajre (1986).

17. Besley (1994); Gonzalez-Vega (1994c).

18. Adams, Graham, and Von Pischke (1984); Kane (1977); Gonzalez-Vega (1993).

19. Gonzalez-Vega and Mesalles-Jorba (1993).

20. Benston and others (1986).

21. Chaves and Gonzalez-Vega (1994).

22. Allocative efficiency requires that available resources flow to the financial organizations that offer the highest expected risk-adjusted rates of return. Regulation should not be used to promote the achievement of *social* objectives or to assist particular sectors of the population for reasons not related to the services of financial intermediation per se.

23. Camacho-Castro and Gonzalez-Vega (1994).

24. Kane (1977; 1985).

25. Von Pischke (1991).

26. Kane (1984); Von Pischke (1991).

27. With imperfect intertemporal markets and information asymmetries, initially unequal allocations of assets (such as land) may have long-lasting adverse consequences on efficiency and growth through their implications for the ability to accumulate physical and human capital. However, government policies to deal with these problems have aggravated rather than alleviated the credit rationing of poor people. Bencivenga and Smith (1991).

28. Gonzalez-Vega and Graham (1995).

29. Stiglitz and Weiss (1981); Rashid and Townsend (1994).

30. Besley (1994).

31. Gonzalez-Vega (1993).

32. Mynt (1992).

33. Stiglitz and Weiss (1981).

34. Holmstrom (1993).

35. Gonzalez-Vega (1994b).

36. Chaves and Gonzalez-Vega (1996).

37. Krahnen and Schmidt (1994).

38. Gonzalez-Vega and Graham (1995).

39. Chaves and Gonzalez-Vega (1994).

40. Vittas (1992).

41. Trigo (1996).

42. Poyo, Gonzalez-Vega, and Aguilera-Alfred (1993).

43. Chaves and Gonzalez-Vega (1994).

Chapter 11

DIMITRI VITTAS

Social Security, Pension, and Insurance Reform in Developing Economies

In this chapter I discuss the sequencing of social security, pension, and insurance reform in developing countries. For both economic and regulatory reasons, most developing countries have underdeveloped pension funds and insurance sectors; meanwhile, their social security systems face many financial and organizational problems. Wide-ranging social security, pension, and insurance reform has considerable potential economic and social benefits. A restructured social security system would avoid financial insolvency and be better able to meet its redistributive objectives. The development of pension funds and insurance business could generate large amounts of long-term financial resources, thereby stimulating the growth of capital markets and enabling these entities to provide adequate and affordable long-term benefits to members and policyholders.

The chapter is divided into sections that address underdevelopment of contractual savings and insurance in developing countries; the state of social security in different countries; the benefits of reform in social security systems; and the desirability and applicability of the sequencing strategy for social security reform. My discussion of sequencing focuses on restructuring and downsizing social pensions, creating a multipillar structure, streamlining the regulatory framework, and formulating a transition plan.

DETERMINANTS OF UNDERDEVELOPMENT

Except for a few countries such as Chile, Fiji, Malaysia, Singapore, and South Africa (and to a lesser degree Cyprus, Egypt, Korea, and Zimbabwe), most developing countries have small contractual savings sectors. In the vast majority of developing countries, the assets of pension funds and insurance companies correspond to less than 10 percent of gross domestic product (GDP); in the countries listed above and in several developed countries they exceed 30 percent, and in some cases more than 70 percent of GDP. The most important reason for the underdevelopment of contractual savings and insurance business in developing countries is the low level of income and wealth. Poor households cannot afford to put aside large sums of money for their future needs, and households with few possessions have less need for property and casualty insurance.

Although high-growth countries have a high rate of saving, such saving is usually first placed in bank deposits and other liquid instruments. Only after income and savings reach a reasonably high level is money typically put aside for retirement and old age benefits. Similarly, the insurance habit of covering property and casualty losses starts to spread only after people acquire substantial possessions and become concerned about the effects of accidental losses. In most developing countries, poor households live in rural areas where elderly people depend on the support of their extended families. There is therefore less need for saving through formal institutions, such as insurance companies and pension funds. But as the extended families break up under the pressures of economic growth and urbanization, the need for alternative arrangements clearly increases.

However, not all developing countries have such low income and wealth. Many have incomes and wealth that would justify a strong demand for contractual savings outlets and insurance services. What holds back the development of contractual savings and insurance in these countries is often the prevailing macroeconomic environment and regulatory framework. High inflation has a particularly adverse effect. Pension funds and life insurance companies cannot function properly in a highly inflationary environment, unless they are based on fully indexed contracts. But full indexation is problematic in countries with high inflation rates. Nonlife insurance also is hit by high inflation as houses and other assets become easily underinsured (unless contracts are indexed); meanwhile, the cost of claims that insurance companies have to pay becomes difficult to predict and is affected by long delays in settlement. The generally highly burdensome regulatory framework also has a negative impact, because it impedes competition, innovation and efficiency. The insurance sector is often dominated by one or two state-owned companies, while entry into the insurance market by privately owned companies as well as foreign companies is discouraged. Both premiums and new products are subject to vetting and control by regulatory agencies that are rarely staffed with experienced professionals. A major problem is often the imposition of investment rules that force pension funds and insurance companies to invest their assets in government bonds with highly negative real rates of return.

The insurance sector of most developing countries is characterized by inadequate capital, low investment returns, high operating costs, and lax control over brokers. Other difficulties include high levels of receivables, fraud, and unduly steep claims by some insured, but otherwise low claims and settlements for the majority of customers; and protracted disputes and long delays in settlement. In most developing countries, there is widespread mutual mistrust between insurance companies and their customers. This is aggravated by the information problems that afflict the insurance industry. Insurance companies therefore impose various restrictions and conditions on their policies to protect themselves from "adverse selection" (that is, having large numbers of ill people among their policyholders), "moral hazard" (or the absence of incentives encouraging people to take measures to prevent accidents from happening), and outright fraud. But such restrictions give rise to disputes and delays in settlement that undermine the public's confidence in the honesty and integrity of insurers, causing a decline in the demand for insurance services. This widespread mistrust affects not only relations with households but also business with both large and small firms. Without proper insurance, industry and commerce suffer from undue exposure to fire and other hazards, and uninsured losses that result can be debilitating for a company.

THE STATE OF SOCIAL SECURITY SYSTEMS

The development of pension funds and life insurance companies is also often adversely affected by social security systems paying or promising to pay generous pension benefits. This is more a problem for middle- and high-income countries; in low-income countries social security systems are less well developed, and where they exist they usually have very limited coverage. Apart from discouraging the development of long-term contractual savings, the social security systems of most developing countries also have their own internal financial and structural problems. These cause considerable distortions in incentives and allocation of resources and cast doubt on the systems' long-term viability.

Much has been written recently about the pressing problems of social security systems in Latin American and eastern European countries.[1] Considerable attention has also been focused on the problems caused by the progressive aging of the populations of developing countries. (However, demographic aging in most developing countries is by no means a current problem, but rather a potential future problem of the second half of the next century.) In fact, the current difficulties facing the social security systems of developing countries stem from major faults in design and implementation and have little to do with the heavy burden imposed by an aged population and aging labor force.

Most developing countries have young populations (in some cases very young), where children represent more than half the total population. These countries should be able to operate their social security systems with low contribution rates. But they have design features that encourage evasion—income understatement when contributors are young and overstatement as they near retirement or take early retirement or "disability." These design faults cause total revenues from contributions to be lower and total payments for benefits higher than what they should be and often result in high required contribution rates for break-even costs.

Extensive evasion as well as early retirement and disability cause the system's dependency ratio to exceed the demographic old-age dependency ratio by a big margin. For instance, in Argentina and Hungary the system dependency ratio is nearly double the demographic dependency ratio, whereas in advanced Organization for Economic Cooperation and Development (OECD) countries, such as Switzerland and Sweden, there is usually a small difference between the two ratios.

Evasion is encouraged, because pensions are not proportional to a worker's years of service, contributions, and lifetime income. Rather, they reflect high accrual rates (2 percent, 4 percent, or even 15 percent) for the first few years of service and a reference income based on earnings in the most recent few years before retirement. In Brazil, for instance, the accrual rate is 15 percent for the first five years, which then drops to 1 percent for the next twenty-five years. When the principle of proportionality is violated, strong incentives are created for strategic manipulation of the system by workers who try to minimize their contributions and maximize their benefits. Strategic manipulation is further encouraged by early retirement provisions and lax conditions for disability pensions. In several countries (including Costa Rica, Hungary, and Uruguay), disability pensions account for more than 25 percent of all pensioners. In most developing countries, the average retirement age is below the normal retirement age.

The social security systems of many countries also have perverse and capricious redistribution. Perverse redistribution occurs when low-income workers subsidize the pensions of high-income workers. Perverse redistribution also occurs when low-income workers in hazardous industries may have shorter life expectancies on retirement than high-income workers in white-collar jobs. But an even more severe problem is the capricious redistribution caused by the impact of inflation. Absent a properly indexed system, large fluctuations in the rate of inflation will cause large variations in initial pensions and in the real value of pension payments over time. Indexing initial pensions (by indexing the definition of reference or base earnings) and pensions in payment may help to reduce the capricious redistribution. However, such indexing will expose the system to strong financial pressures, which will incite further strategic manipulation of the system. Care must be taken to avoid full indexation of the pension system until other problems in the design of the system are corrected.

Most social security systems in developing countries operate on a "pay-as-you-go," unfunded basis. Although many were originally created as funded schemes, over time they were converted de facto or de jure into unfunded schemes, because of highly negative real returns on accumulated balances and an increase in benefits without a commensurate increase in contributions. Unfunded schemes increase the financial burden on current generations of workers; they also cause large intergenerational transfers in those nations with progressive demographic aging. But funded public schemes may not be a sustainable answer, because use of accumulated resources has often been highly inefficient and wasteful.

Negative real returns have been observed in many developing countries with funded public schemes (for example, Egypt and several Anglophone African countries, including Ghana, Nigeria, and Zambia). Real returns have been below −10 percent over long periods of time. Use of social security or provident fund balances as a captive source of funds for financing the government deficit in the face of high inflation rates erodes the real value of these balances and fails to secure long-term financial protection. The exceptions to this general rule have been the provident funds of Malaysia and (to a lesser degree) Singapore and public pension funds in some OECD countries. However, in almost all cases, the returns of private pension funds have been higher than those of public pension funds.

Benefits of Pension Reform

Undoubtedly, the most important benefit is the ability to avert the insolvency of the social security system and thus continue the provision of pension and other long-term benefits. Without reform of the social security and pension system there will be no *adequate and therefore sustainable* benefits. The connection with insurance reform stems from the fact that pension reform often involves an increased demand for term life and disability insurance, as well as for various forms of life annuities. This implies a need for restructuring and modernizing the life insurance industry. The link with nonlife insurance stems from the similarities and close structural links that exist between the two main branches of the insurance industry. One of the claimed benefits of social security and pension reform is the promotion of well-managed and funded schemes that will be able to cope with the problems of demographic aging. Although there is considerable validity to such claims, funding by itself cannot provide a full answer to the problems caused by aging.[2] No one can guarantee that real rates of return will remain higher than growth rates of real earnings with a population that includes a growing number of older people. The rate of saving and funding that might be required could become too large and in some sense self-defeating as higher and higher levels of savings may cause further declines in real returns. The answer to the problem of aging must involve (in some combination) extending the normal retirement age, increasing the mandated contribution (or forced saving) rate, and lowering the targeted replacement rate as well as a greater reliance on funded schemes.

Another potential benefit from social security and pension reform is an increase in the rate of saving that may accompany a move from an unfunded to a largely funded system. In principle, pension funding should lead to a higher saving rate. But in practice there seems to be little correlation between funding levels and saving rates. Anglo-American countries (the United States, the United Kingdom, Canada, Australia, New Zealand, and South Africa) and Scandinavian countries have high levels of pension funding but very low saving rates, while Switzerland, Singapore, and Malaysia have both high levels of funding and high saving rates. In contrast, and to complicate matters further, many countries in western Europe and East Asia with unfunded schemes have long had high saving rates.

The rate of saving is determined by a host of factors, the most important of which are economic growth, fertility, and household access to credit. In addition, the income effect may dominate the substitution effect in pension funding, implying that high real returns on pension fund balances may result in lower annual contributions and thus lower saving rates, given the targeted levels of benefits. In practice, funding can lead to an increased rate of saving if it involves a high rate of forced saving (high contribution rate), low real returns (as the income effect dominates the substitution effect), universal coverage, and limited access to household credit. Although this increase would most likely be transitory, it could still have a beneficial long-term effect if it contributes to higher economic growth, which could then sustain the higher level of saving.

Although the quantitative impact of funded schemes on the rate of saving is debatable, there can be little doubt about its qualitative effects. Pension reform and the promotion of funded schemes cause a large shift in favor of long-term financial savings. They also force people to start saving at a younger age. The availability of substantial amounts of long-term resources has considerable potential benefits for the modernization of capital markets, stimulating financial innovation and improving information disclosure.[3]

It is sometimes argued that pension reform that provides funded schemes should not be undertaken in underdeveloped capital markets. This is a rather shortsighted approach. There is a dynamic inter-action between capital markets and contractual savings institutions, the one reinforcing the growth, efficiency, and modernization of the other. However, promoting funded pension schemes raises some dif-ficult policy questions regarding investment rules and the investment of pension fund assets in overseas securities, small firms, and new ventures. Also, when pension funds and other institutional investors are huge, the question of their role in corporate governance becomes very important. The practical approach is to start with restrictive rules that ensure conservative investment policies. Then the range of oppor-tunities for investing in more risky instruments, including overseas securities, can be expanded as the pension funds increase in size and develop their fund management skills.

Pension and social security reform may also have important, benefi-cial implications for the functioning of labor markets if the incentives for strategic manipulation are removed and any restrictions on labor mobility are substantially weakened. Overall economic efficiency will be enhanced if migration to the informal labor markets is reduced. (However, in many countries strategic manipulation involves under-statement of earnings and extensive use of untaxed fringe benefits, rather than a migration to the informal economy.) Pension reform may also eliminate or at least reduce the occurrence of perverse and capri-cious redistribution and may establish better foundations for achiev-ing modest but desirable redistribution. Under a reformed pension system, contributions will likely be perceived as deferred income rather than as a payroll tax.

Pension and social security reform must grapple with other import-ant issues that have substantial operational implications. For instance, funded schemes are usually supported with fiscal incentives involv-ing tax deferral on any amount of contractual saving. In this respect, tax credits could involve lower tax expenditures and weaker regres-sive effects than income deductions. Promoting systems that minimize operating costs while maximizing real returns, or at least achieving sufficiently high real returns, is as essential as it is difficult to attain. A vexing issue relates to the functioning of annuities markets, which in almost all countries have problems of adverse selection, information deficiencies, uncertainty, and high selling costs. Making the purchase of some efficient type of annuity compulsory (for example, indexed or variable, term-certain, joint, and last survivor annuity) may be a necessary component of a mandated funded pension system.

Finally, creating a strong demand for term life and disability insurance among active workers and of annuity products among retiring workers might accompany pension and social reform. Reforming the insurance sector may be as important for the success of pension reform as the resolution of funding, tax, and investment issues.

SEQUENCING OF REFORMS

One of the most vexing issues facing any type of reform is whether and how to sequence particular reform measures. Clearly, the answer must differ from country to country and must take into account local circumstances, not least of which is the political feasibility of particular measures. Advisers often pay lip service to such country-specific factors and then propose an optimal path for reform that disregards local concerns. The alternative (and more practical) approach is to bring about reform wherever feasible and to work to complete the reform program as conditions become ripe for change. Because local conditions almost never permit optimality in the path of reform, countries follow the second and more practical approach.

Nevertheless, it is important to emphasize that the potential benefits of a reform program will not be fully realized until such an undertaking is completed. Doing things in a less than optimal order may increase the costs of transition and may considerably delay attaining the full benefits of reform. On the other hand, if political and social conditions are not ripe for some reform measures, waiting until they become more conducive to reform may also be quite costly. There is one reform measure that should not be undertaken out of order. This is the indexation of pensions in payment before other measures are taken to restructure and downsize the public pillar. *Indexing the pension system prematurely is a recipe for certain financial disaster.* Yet many countries—from Italy and Greece to Argentina, Poland, and Hungary—have indexed pensions prematurely and suffered the adverse consequences.

The various reform measures I present in this chapter are divided into four sets of actions. The implied optimal order is to first restructure and downsize the existing public pensions, to establish a multipillar structure with both mandatory and voluntary aspects, then to streamline the regulatory framework for pension funds and insurance companies, and finally to implement a long-term transition plan. In many countries, steps two and three precede step one.

Several transitional economies in eastern Europe, most notably Hungary and the Czech Republic, appear to be following this latter approach.[4] The main reason seems to be the lack of political support for a wide-ranging reform of social security and the need to maintain broad political support for the more urgent task of enterprise restructuring. However, the scope of supplementary pension funds and especially for a large increase in their role will remain limited so long as social security contributions continue to be as high as 60 percent of wages (as they are in Hungary). No amount of tax incentives can overcome this problem, except for that part of income of high-salary workers that is not subject to social security contributions.

To reduce the size of unfunded future pension liabilities and limit the opportunities for strategic manipulation of the system, a series of reforms of the existing public pillar is often necessary.

LINK NORMAL RETIREMENT AGE TO LIFE EXPECTANCY AT RETIREMENT. The basic idea is to aim for fifteen to twenty years of average life expectancy in retirement. Extending the retirement age often faces strong opposition from both older and younger workers, because it is widely believed that delaying the retirement of older workers will deprive young workers of jobs. However, there is little evidence that a low normal retirement age plus early retirement schemes could contribute generally to higher employment among young workers.

ELIMINATE PREFERENTIAL TREATMENT OF SOME TYPES OF WORKERS. For example, in many countries, female civil servants with children are entitled to retire with a full pension after only fifteen or twenty years of service.

TIGHTEN CONDITIONS OF ELIGIBILITY FOR DISABILITY PENSIONS AND FOR EARLY RETIREMENT. Streamlining disability pensions is a critical challenge and usually requires independent medical committees to approve disability pensions on objective, clearly specified criteria. With regard to early retirement, appropriate actuarial adjustments (with decrements for early retirement and increments for late retirement) could be introduced. These could help overcome political hostility to the idea of extending the normal retirement age. As a corollary, countries should use longer averaging periods for determining initial pensions. If past records have been kept in good order, two or three years could be added every year to the definition of the base until full career earnings are taken into account. If past records are deficient, one year could be added each year. To maintain the real value of past earnings, yearly nominal earnings could be adjusted by an appropriate earnings index, or a points system could be used (one which credits points for every year of service and amounts to the same thing as indexing nominal earnings). Countries should also use proportionality principle and linear accrual rates to calculate initial pensions, including minimum ones. Governments should consider having a system that is based both on years of contributions and level of average indexed lifetime earnings.

LOWER THE TARGETED REPLACEMENT RATE TO A MORE AFFORDABLE LEVEL. Thirty or at most 40 percent of the average economy wage for a worker with average wages and a full career would be adequate and affordable in most countries. The targeted replacement rate could be linked to the system dependency ratio, thus ensuring that the required contribution rate for the public pillar is less than 10 or 12 percent of wages. For instance, if the system dependency ratio is 30 percent, a replacement rate of 40 percent will require a contribution rate of 12 percent for breakeven to be reached. If the system dependency ratio rises to 40 percent with demographic aging, then the targeted replacement rate could be lowered to 30 percent to leave the required contribution rate at 12 percent. If there is a wide dispersion between minimum and maximum pensions, measures can be taken to reduce such dispersion, such as differential ad hoc adjustments for inflation. This will contain the total cost of pensions and also promote redistribution in favor of low-income workers. Measures to reduce dispersion of pensions would be essential where high pensions are not related to a person's history of contributions and are associated with strategic manipulation and other faults in the design of the pension system.

STREAMLINE THE TAX TREATMENT OF PENSIONS AND CONTRIBUTIONS. Ideally, contributions should benefit from some advantageous tax treatment, whereas pensions should be subject to income tax as any other source of income. As I have noted, the most equitable and least expensive form of tax advantage is to offer a tax credit to all workers who contribute a given percentage of their income to the pension system. (A version of this approach is used in the Czech Republic and has been proposed for Australia.)[5] In funded pension schemes, investment income should also be exempt from income tax. The contribution rate should be lowered to create room for supplementary private pension funds, whether mandatory or voluntary. Clearly, in countries with high contribution rates, failing to lower them to more reasonable levels would severely limit the scope of large supplementary schemes.

ADDRESS THE QUESTIONS OF INDEXATION AND FINANCING OF PUBLIC PENSIONS. Preferably, indexation should be limited to the arithmetic mean of the wage and price index. An alternative approach is to index pensions in payment to the nominal wage index less 1.5 or 2 percent, or some other number reflecting a targeted planned reduction in the relative position of pensions vis-à-vis wages. Such indexation would allow pensioners to enjoy the fruits of continued high economic growth, but without exposing the pension system to financial pressures if real wages fall. If participation in the public pillar is near universal, and especially if low-income workers in rural areas are covered, countries should consider financing pensions from general revenues. Otherwise, uncovered workers and consumers in rural areas could end up subsidizing wealthier covered workers in urban areas.

To improve the financing position of the public pillar, measures to fight evasion and improve collections are also necessary. However, such measures should not be seen as a long-term substitute for other reform measures (for example, an unfunded scheme with high targeted replacement rates is not viable in the long run). The administrative capability of social security institutions should be improved and measures to enhance their investment performance undertaken. Such measures should aim to lower administrative costs, which are steep in many countries, and to raise investment returns, which tend to be quite low. But administrative reforms should not be seen as a substitute for overall reform of the pension system.

ESTABLISHING A MIXED PUBLIC-PRIVATE PENSION SYSTEM

The formulation of a long-term plan for the creation of a multipillar structure involves restructuring and downsizing of the public pillar and establishing supplementary private pension systems. The economic argument in favor of a multipillar structure is based on a better alignment of the different pillars with the basic objectives of pension systems—the first pillar for redistribution and the second for saving, and both pillars for insurance. The practical argument is that there is considerable uncertainty about the robustness of different pillars over the long run. We know that unfunded public pensions alone cannot provide the answer, but we do not know yet whether fully funded private pension systems can do so. This suggests that a policy of diversifying across providers would make good practical sense, at least until there is enough evidence that the funded private pillar can be stable, robust, and efficient in the long run. A number of issues would need to be covered in establishing a multipillar structure.[6] First, a set of structural concerns is important. Should the public pillar take the form of state guarantees for a minimum pension, as in Chile; or a two-part structure, as in Switzerland; or a flat benefit for all workers, as in the Netherlands and, more recently, Argentina; or a means-tested universal benefit for all residents, as in South Africa? Each has advantages and disadvantages that invite careful consideration. The role of state guarantees, not only for minimum pensions but also for the solvency of pension fund managers and insurance companies, would need to be addressed in this context.

CREATE A MANDATORY OR VOLUNTARY SECOND PILLAR. This requires deciding on the voluntary or mandatory nature of the second pillar and defining its coverage, minimum level of contribution, tax treatment, and extent of choice by workers.

CHOOSE BETWEEN EMPLOYER-BASED AND NONEMPLOYER-BASED SCHEMES. The latter are generally fully funded, fully vested, fully portable, and based on individual capitalization schemes. Employer-based schemes may also be based on so-called defined benefit or final salary schemes. The main advantage of such schemes is the offer of retirement income insurance by employers, though this is conditional on continued employment with the same employer as well as on the integrity and solvency of the sponsoring employer.[7] Collective capitalization is usually involved. The schemes may suffer from inadequate funding and unreasonable limitations on vesting and portability that may unduly restrict labor mobility and lead to inequitable treatment among workers.

CONSIDER USE OF VARIABLE CONTRIBUTION RATES TO OVERCOME CON-
CERN ABOUT PASSING THE INVESTMENT AND REPLACEMENT RISK TO
WORKERS. Variable contribution rates could be reset periodically and
on a voluntary basis to achieve a certain targeted replacement rate
once past and projected salary growth and investment income are
taken into account.

CHOOSE BETWEEN CENTRALIZED AND DECENTRALIZED MANAGEMENT.
The former achieves lower operating costs but may show low investment returns. The latter, if based on nonemployer schemes, may have
high selling and other operating costs. Of course, what matters most is
the net investment return, which tends to be higher among decentralized schemes. A compromise is either to authorize employer-based
schemes based on individual capitalization accounts or to combine
centralized management of administrative functions (collection of
contributions, payment of pensions, maintenance of records, dispatch
of statement, and so on) with decentralized management of investment funds. Opting for centralized management would clearly require administrative reform of existing institutions, or establishment
of new ones, to undertake the centralized functions.

REQUIRE TERM LIFE AND DISABILITY INSURANCE. To ensure that the
families of active workers are fully protected from financial loss resulting from the death or disability of their relative, these two types of
insurance should be mandated by the system. Administrators of pension schemes should be required to offer the same terms and conditions for all workers through the purchase or establishment of appropriate group policies. Term life and disability insurance represent
defined benefits in what would otherwise be defined contribution
schemes. Their pricing requires careful actuarial assessments and periodic reviews.

REQUIRE ANNUITIZATION OF BENEFITS OR USE OF SCHEDULED GRADU-
ATED WITHDRAWALS. To ensure that retired workers have sufficient
funds for their old age and avoid outliving their savings, one of two
options should be pursued. Either the purchase of suitable annuities
should be mandated, or withdrawals from the accounts should be
gradual and subject to a well-defined schedule that takes account of
the life expectancy of the workers and their surviving beneficiaries.
The rules for any lump-sum benefits on retirement should be clearly
specified.

STREAMLINING THE
REGULATORY FRAMEWORK

As I have already noted, one of the traditional arguments against funded schemes in developing countries was the absence of efficient, stable, well-regulated, and robust financial systems. Even in developed countries, the historical instability of financial systems was a basic reason for the emergence and growth of unfunded (or, at most, partially funded) social security systems. But in the post–World War II period financial systems have become much more stable and robust and financial regulation and supervision much more sophisticated and effective, even though financial crises and setbacks have not been fully eliminated.

To be effective, social security, pension, and insurance reform in developing countries requires extensive streamlining of the regulatory framework. This should cover not only the providers of pension and insurance products, but also the providers of other financial services (such as payment services) and the securities markets. Support services in the legal, accounting, and auditing spheres must also be streamlined and modernized. The pace of modernization and regulatory reform in securities markets and support services could of course be reinforced by creating large pension fund and insurance sectors. However, parallel and gradual progress on several fronts is essential for the ultimate success of the broader reform program.

With regard to the providers of pension and insurance products, regulatory reform should cover creating or reorganizing regulatory agencies, establishing objective authorization criteria, applying sound solvency and investment rules, and introducing appropriate information disclosure and consumer protection standards. The role of state guarantees would also be a major aspect of the regulatory framework.

CREATE OR REORGANIZE REGULATORY AGENCIES. In many developing countries, regulators have traditionally been concerned with verifying compliance with arbitrary price and product controls rather than with promoting efficient, contestable markets. The new or reorganized agencies must emphasize market discipline, solvency monitoring, and consumer protection and employ experienced professionals. Extensive training may be required, and consultation and cooperation with market practitioners would also be essential.

STRENGTHEN SUPERVISION AND INTERVENTION POWERS OF REGULA-TORS. To ensure the stability of the system and compliance with solvency, investment, and consumer protection rules, regulators must exercise effective supervision through both off-site surveillance and on-site inspection. They also need effective intervention powers to enforce corrective measures.

ESTABLISH OBJECTIVE CRITERIA FOR ENTRY AND EXIT. These should set out the authorization criteria for insurance companies and pension fund managers, establish rules for the exit of insolvent entities, open the market to new domestic and foreign competition, and generally aim to create a contestable but stable market. This may imply a sufficiently but not prohibitively high minimum capital requirement.

DEVELOP SOLVENCY RULES AND RELY ON SOLVENCY MONITORING RATHER THAN PRODUCT AND PRICE CONTROLS. The rules should specify the required solvency margins and capital reserves in relation to total income and assets of individual institutions. They should also emphasize solvency monitoring, both by the regulators and by actuaries, auditors, and other professionals employed by individual institutions. It is also important to encourage reasonable access to international reinsurance markets by eliminating or reducing local retention ratios and applying prudential norms to avoid excessive reinsurance.

APPLY INVESTMENT RULES THAT UNDERSCORE PROFITABILITY AND SAFETY AND PROMOTE DIVERSIFICATION STRATEGIES. Such rules should involve maximum limits and avoid imposing minimum requirements that often result in the use of pension and insurance reserves as a captive source for funding budget deficits. Investment rules should become more liberal as financial markets become more sophisticated and mature. These rules should aim to adopt the "prudent man" rule prevalent in Anglo-American countries. Diversification of investments into overseas securities should also be contemplated—perhaps in keeping with the size and structure of the local market. A country with a small, undiversified market would need to authorize a higher limit for overseas assets than a country with a large, diversified market.

ESTABLISH DETAILED REPORTING AND INFORMATION DISCLOSURE AS WELL AS CONSUMER PROTECTION STANDARDS. Pension contracts have a long time span—up to sixty years: forty in active employment and twenty in retirement. Life insurance contracts also have long terms, exceeding ten years and reaching forty years in the case of pension-linked contracts. For this reason, adequate and meaningful information disclosure is important, as is protection of workers and policyholders.

CONSIDER THE APPROPRIATE ROLE FOR STATE GUARANTEES. Because of their long time span and the economic uncertainties that may affect returns of different entities and products, governments are often forced to provide state guarantees to workers and policyholders. These may cover provision of minimum pensions, or they may protect workers and policyholders against institutional insolvency. The scope and financing of state guarantees would be important ingredients of the whole reform program. But care should be taken to avoid undermining the financial disciplines of market-based funded schemes, thereby inadvertently or indirectly making the system revert to an unfunded pay-as-you-go one.

CONCLUSIONS

I have briefly discussed the sequencing of social security, pension, and insurance reform and have done little more than provide a short and far from exhaustive checklist of what needs to be done regarding these complex issues. I have also briefly reviewed the benefits of reform.

In conclusion, it is perhaps important to underscore the basic objectives of an ambitious reform program:

—Avoid the insolvency of the social security system (this is a longer-run problem for developing countries with young populations), thus ensuring that adequate but affordable (and therefore sustainable) pension benefits will be provided.

—Remove incentives that encourage strategic manipulation and hamper the efficient functioning of labor markets.

—Control perverse and capricious redistribution by removing the many design faults that currently afflict security systems in most developing countries.

—Generate long-term financial savings that can help stimulate the modernization and growth of capital markets, finance long-term investments, and facilitate the privatization program.

Although there is no single optimal way of sequencing and pacing a reform program, the full benefits of the reform will not be realized until existing social pension systems are restructured and downsized, contribution rates lowered, and the scope for private pension funds (whether voluntary or mandatory) increased. However, one imperative that is often ignored is to defer an indexation of the pension system until extensive design faults are corrected. Finally, insurance sector reform is essential for the success of the whole program because of the close links between pension reform and the provision of life, disability, and annuity insurance services.

REFERENCES

Arrau, Patricio, and Klaus Schmidt-Hebbel. 1994. "Pension Systems and Reforms: Country Experiences and Research Issues." *Revista de Analisis Económico* 9 (1): 3–20.

Arrau, Patricio, Salvador Valdes-Prieto, and Klaus Schmidt-Hebbel. 1993. *Privately Managed Pension Systems: Design Issues and the Chilean Experience.* World Bank, mimeo.

Barr, Nicholas. 1992. "Economic Theory and the Welfare State: A Survey and Interpretation." *Journal of Economic Literature* 30 (June): 741–803.

Bodie, Zvi. 1990a. "Pension Funds and Financial Innovation." *Financial Management* 19 (Autumn): 11–22.

_____ . 1990b. "Pensions as Retirement Income Insurance." *Journal of Economic Literature* 28 (March): 28–49.

Davis, E. Philip. 1993. *The Structure, Regulation and Performance of Pension Funds in Nine Industrial Countries.* Policy Research Working Paper 1229. World Bank.

Demirguc-Kunt, Asli, and Anita Schwarz. 1994. *Pension Reform in Costa Rica.* Policy Research Working Paper 1483. World Bank.

Diamond, Peter, and Salvador Valdes-Prieto. 1994. "Social Security Reform." In *The Chilean Economy: Policy Lessons and Challenges*, edited by Barry Bosworth, 257–328. Brookings.

Fox, Louise. 1994. *Old Age Security in Transition Economies.* Policy Research Working Paper 1257. World Bank.

Kane, Cheikh T. 1995a. *Uruguay: Options for Pension Reform.* ESP Discussion Paper Series 68. World Bank.

_____ . 1995b. *Peru: Reforming the Pension System.* ESP Discussion Paper Series 69. World Bank.

Mesa-Lago, Carmelo. 1989. *Ascent to Bankruptcy: Financing Social Security in Latin America.* University of Pittsburgh Press.

McGreevey, William. 1990. *Social Security in Latin America: Issues and Options for the World Bank.* Discussion Paper 110. World Bank.

Queisser, Monika. 1991. "Social Security Systems in Southeast Asia: Indonesia, the Philippines and Singapore." *International Social Security Review* 44 (January/February): 121–35.

———. 1995. "Chile and Beyond: The Second-Generation Pension Reforms in Latin America." *International Social Security Review* 48 (3–4): 23–39.

Schmidt-Hebbel, Klaus. 1994. *Colombia's Pension Reform: Fiscal and Macroeconomic Implications.* World Bank, mimeo.

Vittas, Dimitri. 1992. *Contractual Savings and Emerging Securities Markets.* Policy Research Working Paper 858. World Bank.

———. 1993a. *Swiss Chilanpore: The Way Forward for Pension Reform?* Policy Research Working Paper 1093. World Bank.

———. 1993b. *The Simple(r) Algebra of Pension Plans.* Policy Research Working Paper 1145. World Bank.

———. 1993c. *Options for Pension Reform in Tunisia.* Policy Research Working Paper 1154. World Bank.

———. 1995. *Policies to Promote Saving for Retirement: Tax Incentives or Compulsory Provision?* World Bank, Financial Sector Development Department, mimeo.

Vittas, Dimitri, and Augusto Iglesias. 1992. *The Rationale and Performance of Personal Pension Plans in Chile.* Policy Research Working Paper 867. World Bank.

Vittas, Dimitri, and Roland Michelitsch. 1995. *Pension Funds in Central Europe and Russia: Their Prospects and Potential Role in Corporate Governance.* Policy Research Working Paper 1459. World Bank.

World Bank. 1994. *Averting the Old Age Crisis: Policies to Protect the Old and Promote Growth.* Oxford University Press.

NOTES

1. For a comprehensive worldwide review of social security issues, see World Bank (1994). For more specific discussions of the experience of individual countries or regions, see Arrau and Schmidt-Hebbel (1994); Arrau, Valdes-Prieto, and Schmidt-Hebbel (1993); Davis (1993); Diamond and Valdes-Prieto (1994); Demirguc-Kunt and Schwarz (1994); Fox (1994); Kane (1995a, 1995b);

Mesa-Lago (1989); McGreevey (1990); Queisser (1991, 1995); Schmidt-Hebbel (1994); Vittas (1993c); Vittas and Iglesias (1992); Vittas and Michelitsch (1995).

2. Barr (1992); Vittas (1993b).

3. Bodie (1990a); Davis (1993).

4. Vittas and Michelitsch (1995).

5. Vittas and Michelitsch (1995); Vittas (1995).

6. A fuller discussion of the issues raised by multipillar structures is contained in World Bank (1994). See also Vittas (1993a) for a discussion of the benefits of combining the strong points of different pillars.

7. Bodie (1990b).

Chapter 12

MAXWELL J. FRY

Financial Sector Development in Small Economies

The World Bank lists one hundred economies of nations with populations of less than 4.5 million.[1] In this chapter I examine the question of whether such economies share particular characteristics that suggest alternative sequencing of or differing policy emphases in programs of financial sector development and reform. For some small economies, this question is irrelevant, because they have fully liberalized financial sectors (Ireland, Norway, and Singapore) or form part of a fully liberalized currency bloc (the Channel Islands, Kiribati, and Panama). Nevertheless, for many small economies the issues of sequencing and strategies for financial sector development are highly relevant.

To make this task manageable, I chose a sample of small economies with populations of 500,000 to 1.5 million. Table 12-1 compares some key macroeconomic characteristics of the fourteen sample economies (Bahrain, Botswana, Comoros, Cyprus, Fiji, Gabon, the Gambia, Guinea-Bissau, Guyana, Kuwait, Mauritius, Qatar, Swaziland, and Trinidad and Tobago) with populations between 500,000 and 1.5 million in 1992 with those of fifteen larger economies (Bangladesh, Brazil, Egypt, Ethiopia, Indonesia, Korea, Mexico, Myanmar, Nigeria, Pakistan, Philippines, South Africa, Thailand, Turkey, and Zaire) with populations between 40 million and 200 million.

The population range of 500,000 to 1.5 million contains 17 economies; however, Bhutan, Djibouti, and Réunion were dropped from the sample because of data deficiencies, and Vietnam was dropped from the sample of larger countries for the same reason.

Both economic growth and inflation rates are higher in the large-economy sample than in the small-economy one. Corresponding to the higher inflation rate is a lower money-to-income ratio ($M2$ as a percentage of gross national product [GNP]) in the larger countries.

167

TABLE 12-1. *Macroeconomic Characteristics in Fourteen Small and Fifteen Large Developing Economies*

Averages over the period 1985–92

Variable	Small	Large
Per capita income	$4,200	$1,400
Inflation	11.3	130.4
Growth rate	2.9	3.9
Openness	115.8	44.4
Investment ratio	26.1	21.2
Saving ratio	16.9	16.7
Money/income ratio	57.7	43.5
Foreign debt ratio	138.3	62.9
Government deficit ratio	8.5	4.6

SOURCE: World Bank. 1994. *Socioeconomic Time-Series Access and Retrieval System: World Tables 1994.* Washington: World Bank.

However, the average money income ratio MY over the period 1985–92 is related positively to per capita income, the openness of the economy (exports plus imports as a percentage of GNP), the government deficit as a percentage of GNP, and the size of the economy. Although it is no surprise to find that the small-economy sample is more open than the large-economy one, it might not have been predicted that the small-economy sample would post a foreign debt-to-GNP ratio twice that of the large-economy one. The higher foreign debt corresponds to considerably larger current account deficits in the small economies. In turn, higher current account deficits correspond to higher investment in the small-economy sample; saving ratios are virtually identical. Government deficits are also considerably higher in the small economies.

ENDOGENOUS GROWTH

Combining growth rates and investment ratios indicates that the large-economy sample averaged an incremental output-to-capital ratio of 0.18 compared with 0.11 for the small-economy sample. Lower growth despite higher investment ratios in the small economies is predicted by endogenous growth models. As Krugman notes, "The basic idea of this literature is that there may be external economies to capital accumulation, so that the true elasticity of output with respect to capital greatly exceeds its share of GNP at market prices."[2] To ensure competitive markets in these models, individual firms face declining returns to scale and diminishing marginal productivity of their own capital. However, positive production externalities from the knowledge component or learning process of capital increase returns and raise the marginal productivity of capital at the aggregate level.

An estimate of the average rate of economic growth over the period 1985–92 indicates that higher growth is associated with greater openness, the rate of change in the terms of trade, and the natural logarithm of the economy's population. Lower growth is associated with a higher ratio of foreign debt to GNP and a reduced current account balance in relation to GNP.

This suggests that small economies may gain more from integration with the rest of the world than large economies. Reducing barriers such as capital account constraints may thus stimulate growth more in small than in large economies. Perhaps the capital account should be therefore liberalized as soon as possible, regardless of conditions in the domestic financial system.

FOREIGN DEBT ACCUMULATION

Table 12-1 suggests that, in relation to GNP, small economies may find it easier to borrow abroad than large economies. This may counter the case for more rapid capital account liberalization; easier borrowing enables an economy to relax its fiscal discipline without incurring the normal inflationary consequences. Furthermore, it may raise the foreign debt ratio to a level at which capital flight is stimulated and growth is reduced.[3] The problem of an excessive buildup in foreign debt is that the effective cost at which foreign saving begins to be supplied in any particular year depends on the economy's debt position (inherited from past borrowing). The effective cost of foreign borrowing is also the effective domestic real interest rate.

At a relatively low real interest rate, domestic investment exceeds national saving. The inflow of foreign saving is positive, and the economy runs a current account deficit on its balance of payments. Other things being equal, the accumulation of debt resulting from the current account deficit will reduce foreign saving, thus raising the domestic real interest rate. The result will be less total saving, requiring an increase in the interest rate to restore equilibrium between saving and investment. In this case, foreign debt accumulation reduces domestic investment and raises national saving through a higher domestic real interest rate. The current account deficit declines until it reaches a steady-state equilibrium in which the debt-to-GNP ratio is constant. This interest rate or financial effect explains the positive effect of foreign debt on the U.S. current account detected by Masson, Kremers, and Horne and by Wickens and Uctum. Foreign indebtedness eventually improves the current account and so reverses or reduces the debt buildup.[4]

In developing economies, much of the foreign debt takes the form of government and government-guaranteed foreign debt. The level of this type of foreign debt accumulated from past current account deficits may affect both national saving and domestic investment through another channel. As households notice that government and government-guaranteed foreign debt is rising, they may well anticipate higher future tax burdens to service it. They will therefore have an increasing incentive to transfer assets abroad. David Ricardo foresaw this result almost two centuries ago:

> A country which has accumulated a large debt is placed in a most artificial situation; and although the amount of taxes, and the increased price of labour, may not . . . place it under any other disadvantage with respect to foreign countries, except the unavoidable one of paying those taxes, yet it becomes the interest of every contributor to withdraw his shoulder from the burthen, and to shift this payment from himself to another; and the temptation to remove himself and his capital to another country, where he will be exempted from such burthens, becomes at last irresistible. . . . A country which has involved Itself in the difficulties attending this artificial system, would act wisely by ransom-

ing itself from them, at the sacrifice of any portion of its property which might be necessary to redeem its debt.[5]

Savers could also perceive that a high and rising foreign debt ratio may goad the government into stimulating exports, which would involve devaluating the real exchange rate. In this case, the real returns on assets held abroad could be higher than the real returns on domestic assets.

Most developing economies prohibit capital outflows. Much financial investment abroad takes place through overinvoicing imports and underinvoicing exports as a result.[6] This method of removing capital from an economy reduces measured national saving, even in the unlikely event that the true saving level remains constant. In any event, it reduces national savings available to finance domestic investment. A higher value of government plus government-guaranteed foreign debt might be expected to *reduce* national saving through this *fiscal* effect.

The variable representing this foreign debt factor *DETY* is last year's stock of government plus government-guaranteed foreign debt divided by last year's GNP. In addition to its fiscal effect on national saving, *DETY* also determines the domestic real interest rate. A higher debt ratio produces a higher domestic real interest rate, thus increasing national saving. This financial or interest-rate effect on saving could be the opposite of the fiscal effect of *DETY* outlined here. To allow for these conflicting and possibly nonlinear influences of debt on saving, the debt-to-GNP ratio can be used in quadratic form. The debt ratio *DETY* and the debt ratio squared $DETY^2$ can both be included to explain saving behavior.

The magnitude of capital flight caused by a buildup of foreign debt *DETY* can be destabilizing, as it has been in several developing economies. Instead of an increase in foreign debt having the effect of reducing domestic investment and increasing national saving, the foreign debt buildup reduces national saving; the current account deficit increases. Real interest rates can reach astronomical levels, as they have in several developing economies, without reducing the current account deficit. The end result is financial and economic paralysis. This explains a negative effect of foreign debt on the current account—an

172 : Financial Sector Development in Small Economies

increase in government and government-guaranteed foreign debt can worsen it.

An alternative measure of an economy's foreign indebtedness can be estimated by cumulating the current account deficit over time. In this case, the balance of payments definition of the current account must be used, which subtracts unrequited transfers from the measured deficit. The dollar stock of net foreign liabilities can then be converted into domestic currency and expressed as a ratio of GNP. Perhaps these foreign liabilities exert the stabilizing influence of foreign debt buildup. Furthermore, as net foreign liabilities increase and net wealth declines, higher cumulated net foreign liabilities could reduce consumption, thus raising national saving. In other words, these foreign liabilities could have the opposite effect on government and government-guaranteed foreign debt on the current account. The variable representing these net foreign liabilities FLY is last year's stock of cumulated net foreign liabilities converted into domestic currency, divided by last year's GNP.

Higher foreign indebtedness in the form of government and government-guaranteed foreign debt may also deter domestic investment, because it makes higher taxes on domestic assets more likely in the future. Krueger concludes: "When debt-service obligations are high, increasing public resources to service debt will be likely to reduce incentives and resources available to the private sector sufficiently to preclude the necessary investment response."[7] Sachs documents the deleterious effects of the foreign debt buildup on investment in Latin America.[8] However, the foreign debt ratio also serves as a surrogate for the domestic real interest rate. It could also stand in as a proxy for the intensity of nonprice credit rationing imposed by foreign lenders. In such a case, the foreign debt ratio may affect the investment ratio negatively, reflecting a higher cost of investable funds. In practice, one cannot distinguish between the interest rate or financial effect and the fiscal effect of foreign debt buildup on investment.

In its early stages, debt buildup could actually stimulate investment. Entrepreneurs may perceive profitable investment opportunities in export activities as debt service mounts and the government intensifies a drive to raise foreign exchange earnings. Because there could be several different effects of debt on investment, the foreign debt ratio

DETY and the foreign debt ratio squared *DETY*^{2} can both be used to explain investment behavior in empirical analysis.

My estimated current account equations for a sample of twenty-six developing economies over the period 1960–88 show that an increase in the cumulated current account deficit as a ratio of GNP *FLY* improves the current account ratio significantly.[9] In other words, this stock variable exhibits a stabilizing effect. Current account deficits that have cumulated improve account balances in the future. In contrast, however, the ratio of government and government-guaranteed foreign debt to GNP has a significant negative effect on the current account ratio.[10] Current account deficits financed through this type of foreign debt are not self-correcting. A rise in the stock of foreign debt of this type worsens the current account and accelerates its own buildup, perhaps because it stimulates capital flight.

When government and government-guaranteed foreign debt is held constant, an increase in net foreign liabilities as measured by the cumulated balance-of-payments deficit produces self-correcting tendencies—possibly through declining wealth, which reduces consumption and increases saving. In other words, these results corroborate the Masson-Kremers-Horne and Wickens-Uctum findings.[11] In contrast, when the cumulated balance-of-payments deficit is held constant and government and government-guaranteed debt rises, destabilizing forces are unleashed. Direct government and government-guaranteed foreign borrowing have actually financed capital flight in many heavily indebted economies, and the accumulation of such debt has failed to produce a self-correcting wealth effect. Moreover, the accumulation of assets in the heavily indebted economy is made less and less attractive. The policy implication is that, while rapid capital account liberalization could integrate small economies with the rest of the world, thus raising growth rates for any given investment ratio, government deficits should be reduced, along with the curtailment of direct government and government-guaranteed borrowing.

ECONOMIES OF SCALE IN BANKING

Given banking's economies of scale, banking in small economies may well be more costly than in large economies.[12] The effects of variable financial intermediation costs on growth have been examined in the literature, which is complex.[13] King and Levine show that in general equilibrium, there is an ambiguous relationship between the real interest rate r and growth.[14] In Romer's model, the relationship is negative.[15] If households can save only in the form of bank deposits and firms borrow from the banks to finance investment, higher intermediation costs reduce growth. Both Pagano and Sussman have modeled financial development as a process of reducing such costs, thus accelerating the rate of economic growth.[16]

For small economies with high costs of financial intermediation that reduce rates of economic growth, one solution may be to import foreign banks. In examining the financial systems in eleven small island developing economies in 1981, I found that there were more foreign banks than domestic ones operating in nine of these economies (with Hong Kong and Singapore constituting the exceptions).[17] Table 12-2 provides the breakdown in 1981 for these nine economies.

Despite the small number of banks, commercial banks dominated the financial sectors of all these economies. The Bahamas and Papua New Guinea had a few savings and loan associations, the Seychelles had its Government Savings Bank, and there was a Post Office Savings Bank in Western Samoa. These were the only nonbank depository institutions in these nine economies.

Strength and breadth of these financial systems and the size of the economy show a strong correlation. The financial sector of the Maldives, with a 1979 GNP of $30 million, was rudimentary in the extreme. Financial sectors in St. Lucia ($95 million), the Seychelles ($91 million), the Solomon Islands ($96 million), and Western Samoa ($66 million) were just one rung up the ladder. Papua New Guinea ($1,950 million) had a marginally more extensive financial sector, though its per capita income was about half that of the Seychelles. The "big" economies of Hong Kong ($19 billion) and Singapore ($9 billion) possessed financial sectors comparable to any found in the Organization for Economic Cooperation and Development (OECD) economies. The correlation is mainly caused by the economies of scale that exist in financial intermediation.

In unit banking states in the United States, there was one bank for every $65 million of GNP in 1979. However, these banks could share services, such as computer facilities, which enabled them to reap some

TABLE 12-2. *Banks in Nine Small Island Developing Economies, 1981*

Economy	Domestic	Foreign
Bahamas	0	11
Barbados	1	5
Fiji	1	5
Maldives	0	2
Papua New Guinea	1	3
Saint Lucia	1	4
Seychelles	0	6
Solomon Islands	½	2½
Western Samoa	½	1½

SOURCE: Maxwell J. Fry. 1981. "Financial Intermediation in Small Island Developing Economies." Commonwealth Economic Papers 16. London: Commonwealth Secretariat (September), p. 50.

of the benefits of scale economies. Furthermore, they could easily purchase intermediate inputs such as checkbooks from specialized firms supplying the U.S. banking industry as a whole. Labor costs of all insured banks in the United States were 1.6 percent of earning assets in 1976. The comparable figure for Turkey, for example, was 5.8 percent. Unit labor costs of banking in the United States can be presumed to be less than unit labor costs of banking in any small economy. From all this, it might be concluded that a minimum economy size needed to support one viable domestic bank would have been to have a 1979 GNP of at least $100 million. This implies that not even one private domestic bank could have survived without government subsidy in the Maldives, St. Lucia, the Seychelles, the Solomon Islands, and Western Samoa. Based on this estimate, the Bahamas and Barbados could have supported six private domestic banks each, Fiji ten, and Papua New Guinea twenty, provided each had only one branch.

This estimate for Papua New Guinea illustrates the fact that not only is economy size crucial but so is expertise. Qualified personnel to run twenty private domestic banks in Papua New Guinea are just not available there. Even with adequate economy sizes, Afghanistan and Nepal illustrate the problems of establishing and maintaining all-domestic financial sectors without an adequate supply of trained personnel. Specifically, foreign trade financing constituted a serious impediment to foreign trade in these economies. The banks could not be relied upon to execute correctly operations such as opening letters of credit.[18] Foreign banks tend to have strong comparative advantage in terms of expertise and experience in foreign trade financing. For some small economies, deficiencies in economy size, training, and know-how leave no room for choice. Either financial intermediation is undertaken by foreign banks or there will simply be none at all.

Herbert Grubel provides one of the most comprehensive frameworks with which to assess the costs and benefits of permitting foreign banks to establish branches in economies where a choice is possible.[19] The main advantages to be measured are increased competition forced on domestic financial intermediaries that would otherwise form an oligopolistic if not a cartelized industry, importation and use of existing stocks of knowledge capital or know-how at low marginal cost, and increased efficiency of international capital flows.[20] The disadvantages of hosting foreign banks, according to Grubel, may include:

—Exemption from socially beneficial regulations;

—Loss of control over eurodollar liquidity; and

—Inflation created by multiple deposits of eurodollars.[21]

Other disadvantages that should be considered include:

—Inefficiency in resource mobilization and allocation resulting from unfamiliarity with local conditions;

—Export of national saving to the economy of origin, again from unfamiliarity with or unresponsiveness to local conditions;

—Formation of a foreign bank cartel that dictates or thwarts monetary policy measures; and

—Increased difficulty in establishing a new domestic bank when foreign banks are well-established and hold all the best accounts.

The four latter potential disadvantages can be magnified all too easily by inappropriate laws and regulations. Inefficient resource mobilization and allocation is virtually assured if the monetary authority sets binding ceilings on deposit and loan rates of interest. Conversely, permitting and encouraging mobile bank branches, ensuring prompt and effective legal redress in cases of loan delinquencies and defaults, and contributing toward training costs can promote efficient resource mobilization and allocation for both domestic and foreign banks. Charging license fees, as St. Lucia did for both head offices and branches, is likely to reduce efficiency of financial intermediation. Setting minimum deposit rates, as Barbados does, may increase efficiency. No matter how small the number of financial intermediaries, whether domestic or foreign, regulations can be designed and implemented to simulate competitive conditions—for example, by setting minimum deposit rates of interest. Equally important, discriminatory taxation of financial intermediation can and should be avoided in the interests of efficiency. Most measures I have discussed here in connection with increasing or decreasing financial intermediation efficiency also affect the incentive foreign banks have to siphon off national saving to their home economies. Additionally, a rapidly depreciating currency tends to stimulate capital flight.

That foreign bank cartels can indeed influence, if not dictate, monetary policy is illustrated by an event in St. Lucia. In 1980, the government proposed the imposition of a 2 percent tax on banks' deposit liabilities. The proposal was dropped after discussions with the foreign banks. A potential foreign bank cartel can best be averted and existing cartels undermined by relatively free market entry. However, small developing economies could realize substantial savings in the costs of information gathering by granting licenses only to large, reputable foreign banks—those least likely to risk adverse publicity from sharp practices. There might also be some advantages (as the Seychelles recognized in 1976) in inviting foreign banks from several different economies to establish offices.

There seems to be no proven way of solving the problem of subsequent domestic entry into a financial intermediary industry historically the exclusive territory of foreign financial intermediaries. Typically, government ownership has been the method attempted. An alternative technique might be to initially reserve thrift intermediation for domestic enterprise and then to amalgamate the two subsectors. Another alternative would be to issue fixed-term licenses to foreign banks, with an agreement that the intermediary would be transferred to local ownership at the end of the term.

SEQUENCING ISSUES

Caprio points out that "initial conditions matter a great deal in determining the impact of financial sector reforms."[22] These conditions clearly exert a strong influence on the nature and sequencing of whatever financial sector reforms are adopted. Where no urgent and obvious problems exist, as in Japan and Korea, financial sector reform can occur gradually and in some reasonably logical sequence. However, in most cases financial sector reform is triggered by an immediate and urgent problem or by a window of opportunity that may not exist for long.

Perhaps the most prevalent problem of sequencing in practice involves the inevitable adjustments in the initial comprehensive and interrelated reform plans drafted by the technicians. Various components are politically unacceptable, others are resisted by interested parties; the policymakers' caution tends to water down the remaining elements. In such cases, far from worrying about optimal sequencing of reforms, one is left to decide whether no change might not be preferable, rather than the motley assortment of changes remaining in the reform package. As a result, the issue is often not so much sequencing as delineating the minimum conditions under which it would be worthwhile to embark on the reform course at all. After having shown that something works in the desired way, opportunities for introducing further measures may then become available.

Aspects of the sequencing of financial sector reforms have been analyzed systematically by many authors.[23] Sundararajan provides the most detailed list of the components of a financial sector reform that in theory might be sequenced:

1. Reforming the interest rate regime supported by the development of market-based instruments of monetary control.

2. Developing money and interbank markets, again supported by instruments of monetary control such as treasury bill auctions and open market operations.

3. Improving prudential regulation and supervision.

4. Recapitalizing and restructuring insolvent financial institutions.

5. Increasing competition between banks by relaxing entry restrictions, attacking collusion, and privatizing government-owned banks.

6. Reducing and eventually abolishing selective or directed credit policies.

7. Developing long-term capital markets by issuing longer-term government securities and improving securities regulation.

8. Improving the clearing and settlements system for payments.

9. Developing foreign exchange markets by liberalizing foreign exchange and trade restrictions.[24]

But Sundararajan then goes on to caution: "Although theoretically it is possible to conceive of an optimal sequence of reforms, in most developing countries reforms of monetary management to create indirect instruments and development of money markets should be pursued simultaneously. This is because, in practice, there are on the one hand strong policy and operational linkages between the development of interbank money markets and of markets in short-term instruments, and the reforms of monetary management and the development of indirect and market-based instruments of monetary policy on the other. This argument suggests that money market development has to be emphasized early in the reform sequence."[25]

In fact, several other components Sundararajan cited contain such strong linkages that simultaneous action is imperative. For example, many banks become insolvent as a result of bad loans made under directed credit programs. There is therefore little point in recapitalizing and restructuring insolvent financial institutions unless selective or directed credit policies are abolished or at least rationalized.

Although most practitioners would not object to the components listed by Sundararajan, the relative importance of the various elements would undoubtedly vary from country to country. In the least-developed countries, such as Afghanistan, Laos, and Nepal, reform of the clearing and settlements system might be placed at the top of the list. A banking system that cannot transfer funds reliably and speedily within the country is unlikely to be greatly affected by improved money markets. Most of the small economies in the sample selected here, however, do possess financial systems capable of effecting payments. Based on the analysis in this chapter, my priorities for a representative small economy would therefore be as follows.

ENSURE THAT FISCAL DISCIPLINE IS FIRMLY ESTABLISHED. This will help see to it that domestic financial reforms do not exacerbate the inflationary impact of deficit finance and that capital account liberalization does not encourage capital flight. To counter disruptive and excessive capital inflows, the same reserve requirements should be imposed on foreign borrowing as are effectively imposed (through reserve requirements on deposits) on domestic borrowing. In addition, there should be no government guarantees for foreign borrowing, and lengthen maturities of any government borrowing abroad.

IN CONJUNCTION WITH ABOLISHMENT OF EXCHANGE CONTROLS EARLY IN THE REFORM PROCESS, ESTABLISH A MECHANISM FOR DEFENDING THE DOMESTIC CURRENCY AGAINST SPECULATIVE ATTACK. It is particularly noteworthy that overnight money market rates in both Singapore and Switzerland have occasionally reached triple digits. The monetary authorities chose not to meet the reserve demands of the commercial banks over and above predetermined levels. In both cases, however, the monetary authorities managed the exchange rate. The only way that commercial banks collectively could therefore obtain reserves was to borrow abroad and sell the foreign exchange to the monetary authorities. Transactions costs ensured that overnight rates rose to about 120 percent before borrowing abroad for twenty-four hours became as cheap as domestic borrowing.

To avoid the situation exemplified by the Bank of England's attempt at defending sterling in September 1992, the monetary authority must ensure that banks cannot borrow at the back door domestic currency sold to the central bank at the front door. The Bank of England bought sterling from commercial banks wishing to speculate by buying foreign currency. At the same time, it lent this sterling back to the commercial banks to satisfy their liquidity needs at an interest cost that had been increased by a derisory amount (3 percentage points). To prevent no-risk speculation against the domestic currency and to prevent excess monetary expansion, a three-tier overdraft system for commercial banks could be adopted with the central bank. The first or normal overnight overdraft facility might equal the coefficient of variation of each bank's daily deposit level over the past 12 months; the overdraft rate would equal bank rate plus perhaps 1 percent. The second tranche would be available up to the same volume as the first, but at a cost of bank rate plus 50 percent. A third and final tranche would be available at bank rate plus 500 percent.

GIVE HIGH PRIORITY TO IMPROVING EFFICIENCY AND LOWERING TRANSACTION COSTS IN FOREIGN EXCHANGE MARKETS. Small economies exhibit wide spreads between buying and selling rates for their domestic currencies vis-à-vis foreign currencies. Given their heavy reliance on foreign trade, the transaction costs can represent a significant proportion of GNP. Increasing efficiency and holding down transaction costs should therefore be given as high a priority as improving efficiency in domestic financial markets. In very small economies, foreign exchange markets may be improved and forward markets developed more easily if nontourist exchange activities are concentrated in only one foreign currency (typically the U.S. dollar). The development of a reasonably active spot market for the dollar encourages relatively rapid development of forward markets for the dollar. Once these markets are available locally, all other currencies can be accessed in the highly efficient spot and forward markets of the international financial centers.

FOR SMALL ECONOMIES, ESTABLISH AN APEX REGULATORY INSTITUTION TO OVERSEE REGULATION AND SUPERVISION THROUGHOUT THE FINANCIAL SYSTEM. The primary task of the apex institution is to ensure that regulations are uniform and consistent across groups of financial institutions and markets. However, the apex institution might itself economize on scarce supervisory skills by supervising embryonic parts of the financial sector itself, and assisting and coordinating supervisory activities of other subsector regulatory agencies.

TO MAINTAIN MONETARY CONTROL, PARTICULARLY WHEN IT IS LIKELY TO BE STRAINED WITH THE ABOLITION OF EXCHANGE CONTROLS, HAVE MARKET-BASED INSTRUMENTS OF MONETARY POLICY IN PLACE BEFORE CREDIT CEILINGS ARE ABOLISHED. In several economies, including Indonesia in 1983, credit ceilings were abolished with considerable fanfare without any thought given to alternative means of credit control. Auction and open market operation techniques require some experience. As a result, there is considerable advantage in establishing these institutional arrangements, even though they serve little or no monetary control purpose, before dismantling the controls through credit ceilings. Given the technical complexities involved in adopting risk-weighted capital adequacy requirements, it seems essential to ensure that such requirements are being effectively applied before liquid asset, reserve, and loan/deposit ratio requirements are abolished. Competitive forces from abroad certainly dictate that balance sheet ratio restraints have to be removed to ensure that the domestic financial system will not be subject to negative effective protection. Nevertheless, adopting internationally agreed standards of capital adequacy takes more than just an announcement from the authorities.

GIVEN THE EARLY ABOLITION OF EXCHANGE CONTROLS, SMALL ECONO-MIES SHOULD RESIST ANY TEMPTATION TO USE THE EXCHANGE RATE AS A NOMINAL ANCHOR. The exception is if they are prepared to adopt a currency board, as Estonia has done. Worldwide experience (particularly in the case of the Exchange Rate Mechanism of the European Monetary System) indicates that there is no stable halfway house. If a small economy does not want to adopt a currency board or to use the currency of a larger country, it should rely on domestic policies—monetary, fiscal, and possibly wage policies—to ensure price stability and manage the exchange rate to ensure continued export competitiveness.

Under most conditions, this involves maintaining a reasonably stable real exchange rate. The small size of markets and the limited number of market players suggests that proliferation of different types of financial claims should be resisted where possible. For example, there seems to be no good justification for central bank bonds when treasury bills are available. If the Ministry of Finance resists the idea of treasury bill sales in excess of the government's financing requirements, a special account can be established in the central bank. All proceeds from treasury bill sales in excess of the government's financing requirements can be deposited automatically in this account and earn interest equal to the treasury bill yield. In this way, there are no direct financial consequences of the excess sales of treasury bills for the ministry. Furthermore, the central bank can underwrite the tender at treasury bill auctions, thus building a portfolio of bills for future open market operations. The issue of treasury bills over the year can be smoothed, reducing the government's financing costs on average.

GIVEN THE CONSIDERABLE PROBLEMS OF TAX ENFORCEMENT IN SMALL ECONOMIES, ABOLITION OF EXCHANGE CONTROL MIGHT PREFERABLY BE ACCOMPANIED BY SUBSTITUTION OF A CONSUMPTION TAX FOR AN IN-COME TAX. Alternatively, all income from capital (interest and dividend income) could be exempt from tax. Germany's experience with the introduction of a withholding tax on deposit interest demonstrates the difficulty of enforcing a tax on worldwide income. In this case, Luxembourg became awash with deposit money transferred from Germany simply to avoid this tax. The tax was consequently rescinded.

Although experience might suggest that abolishing exchange controls relatively early in the process of financial reform and development would be appropriate advice for many small developing economies in which fiscal discipline had been established, two major questions remain.

The first question is how to curb or counter an explosion in consumer lending after financial liberalization, particularly in the form of the abolition of credit ceilings. The second is how to confront the lemming instinct common to bankers throughout the world. International evidence suggests that easier access to consumer credit lowers private saving ratios in the medium term.[26] A burst of consumer lending following financial liberalization may also jeopardize monetary control or squeeze out investment lending. Perhaps the pragmatic answer lies in imposing high down payment requirements for mortgages and loans for durable consumer goods at the outset of the liberalization program. Subsequently, such requirements can be gradually reduced, particularly when the economy is in no danger of overheating.

The lemming instinct takes the form of bank lending surging into particular sectors or activities, only to withdraw again after delinquency and default rates rise. Many newly liberalized banking systems have become overly enthusiastic about property development, credit card lending, and housing, only to find that expected returns failed to materialize. The macroeconomic problem is that such credit surges produce bubbles in which prices increase solely as a result of the credit injections. When the bubbles burst, banks are left with collateral worth considerably less than the loans that are found to be nonperforming.

One possible solution is to encourage diversification and discourage concentration through a more sophisticated risk assessment for risk-adjusted capital adequacy requirements. In this case, a bank's portfolio would be assessed in terms of the covariance of individual loan default probabilities. The score in this exercise would then produce an adjusted capital adequacy requirement. The main problem is that the internationally agreed system of risk-weighted capital adequacy assessment is already too complicated for many developing economies to implement effectively. Adding even more complexity may have to wait. Meanwhile, the central bank may simply have to resort to the tried and true technique of moral suasion.

REFERENCES

Baltensperger, Ernst. 1972. "Economies of Scale, Firm Size, and Concentration in Banking." *Journal of Money, Credit and Banking* 4 (August): 467—88.

Bisat, Amer, R. Barry Johnston, and Venkataraman Sundararajan. 1992. "Issues in Managing and Sequencing Financial Sector Reforms: Lessons from Experiences in Five Developing Countries." Working Paper WP/92/82. Washington: International Monetary Fund (October).

Blejer, Mario I., and Silvia B. Sagari. 1987. "The Structure of the Banking Sector and the Sequence of Financial Liberalization." In *Economic Reform and Stabilization in Latin America*, edited by Michael Connolly and Claudio Gonzalez-Vega, 93–107. Praeger.

Caprio, Gerard, Jr. 1995. "Banking on Financial Reform? A Sensitive Dependence on Initial Conditions." In *Financial Reform: Theory and Experience*, edited by Gerard Caprio, Jr., and others, 49–65. Cambridge University Press.

Cole, David C., and Betty F. Slade. 1992. "Financial Development in Indonesia." In *The Oil Boom and After: Indonesian Economic Policy and Performance in the Soeharto Era*, edited by Anne Booth, 77–101. Oxford University Press.

Fry, Maxwell J. 1974a. *The Afghan Economy: Money, Finance and the Critical Constraints to Economic Development*. Leiden, Netherlands: Brill.

———. 1974b. *Resource Mobilization and Financial Development in Nepal*. Kathmandu, Nepal: Centre for Economic Development and Administration.

———. 1981. "Financial Intermediation in Small Island Developing Economies." Commonwealth Economic Paper 16. London: Commonwealth Secretariat.

———. 1982. "Financial Sectors in Some Small Island Developing Economies." In *Problems and Policies in Small Economies*, edited by Bimal Jalan, 185–207. London: Croom Helm.

———. 1989. "Foreign Debt Instability: An Analysis of National Saving and Domestic Investment Responses to Foreign Debt Accumulation in 28 Developing Countries." *Journal of International Money and Finance* 8 (September): 315–44.

———. 1993. "Foreign Debt Accumulation: Financial and Fiscal Effects and Monetary Policy Reactions in Developing Countries." *Journal of International Money and Finance* 12 (August): 347–67.

———. 1995. *Money, Interest, and Banking in Economic Development*, 2d ed. Johns Hopkins University Press.

Grubel, Herbert G. 1977. "A Theory of Multinational Banking." *Banca Nazionale del Lavoro Quarterly Review* 123 (December): 349–63.

Jappelli, Tullio, and Marco Pagano. 1994. "Saving, Growth, and Liquidity Constraints." *Quarterly Journal of Economics* 109 (February): 83–109.

King, Robert G., and Ross Levine. 1993. "Finance, Entrepreneurship, and Growth: Theory and Evidence." *Journal of Monetary Economics* 32 (December): 513–42.

Krueger, Anne O. 1987. "Debt, Capital Flows, and LDC Growth." *American Economic Review* 77 (May): 159–64.

Krugman, Paul R. 1993. "International Finance and Economic Development." In *Finance and Development: Issues and Experience*, edited by Alberto Giovannini, 11–23. Cambridge University Press.

Liu, Liang-Yn, and Wing Thye Woo. 1994. "Saving Behaviour under Imperfect Financial Markets and the Current Account Consequences." *Economic Journal* 104 (May): 512–27.

McKinnon, Ronald I. 1993. *The Order of Economic Liberalization: Financial Control in the Transition to a Market Economy*, 2d ed. Johns Hopkins University Press.

Masson, Paul, Jeroen Kremers, and Jocelyn Horne. 1994. "Net Foreign Assets and International Adjustment: The United States, Japan, and Germany." *Journal of International Money and Finance* 13 (February): 27–40.

Pagano, Marco. 1993. "Financial Markets and Growth: An Overview." *European Economic Review* 37 (April): 613–22.

Patrick, Hugh T. Forthcoming. "Comparisons, Contrasts and Implications." In *Financial Development of Japan, Korea and Taiwan*, edited by Hugh T. Patrick and Yung Chul Park. Oxford University Press.

Ricardo, David. 1817. *On the Principles of Political Economy, and Taxation*. London: John Murray.

Romer, Paul. 1990. "Endogenous Technological Change." *Journal of Political Economy* 98 (October): S71–S102.

———. 1991. "Increasing Returns and New Developments in the Theory of Growth." In *Equilibrium Theory and Applications: Proceedings of the Sixth International Symposium in Economic Theory and Econometrics*, edited by William A. Barnett and others, 83–110. Cambridge University Press.

Sachs, Jeffrey D. 1986. "Managing the LDC Debt Crisis." *Brookings Papers on Economic Activity* (2): 397–431.

Sundararajan, Venkataraman. 1992. "Financial Sector Reforms and Their Appropriate Sequencing." Washington: International Monetary Fund, Monetary and Exchange Affairs Department (September).

Sussman, Oren. 1993. "A Theory of Financial Development." In *Finance and Development: Issues and Experience*, edited by Alberto Giovannini, 29–57. Cambridge University Press.

Watson, C. Maxwell. 1993. "Financial Liberalization and the Economic Adjustment Process." Washington: International Monetary Fund (January).

Wickens, Michael, and Merih Uctum. 1993. "The Sustainability of Current Account Deficits: A Test of the U.S. Intertemporal Budget Constraint." *Journal of Economic Dynamics and Control* 17 (May): 423–41.

World Bank. 1994. *Socioeconomic Time-Series Access and Retrieval System: World Tables 1994.* Washington: World Bank.

NOTES

1. World Bank (1994).
2. Krugman (1993, p. 17).
3. Fry (1993).
4. Masson, Kremers, and Horne (1994); Wickens and Uctum (1993).
5. Ricardo (1817, p. 338).
6. An exporter submits an invoice for a smaller sum than that actually received for the exports when surrendering foreign exchange to the central bank. The difference can then be deposited in the exporter's bank account abroad. Conversely, an importer submits an invoice for an amount exceeding the true cost of the imports to siphon the difference into a foreign bank account.
7. Krueger (1987, p. 163).
8. Sachs (1986, pp. 416–18).
9. Fry (1993, p. 364).
10. Fry (1989, p. 326; 1993, p. 364).
11. Masson, Kremers, and Horne (1994); Wickens and Uctum (1993).
12. Baltensperger (1972).
13. Fry (1995, p. 72).
14. King and Levine (1993, pp. 523–27).
15. Romer (1990).
16. Pagano (1993); Sussman (1993).
17. Fry (1981; 1982).
18. Fry (1974a, chs. 5 and 8; 1974b).
19. Grubel (1977).
20. Grubel (1977, pp. 357–58).
21. Grubel (1977, p. 358).
22. Caprio (1995).

23. Bisat, Johnston, and Sundararajan (1992); Blejer and Sagari (1987); Cole and Slade (1992); McKinnon (1993); Sundararajan (1992); Watson (1993).
24. Sundararajan (1992, pp. 6–7).
25. Sundararajan (1992, p. 8).
26. Jappelli and Pagano (1994); Liu and Woo (1994); Patrick (forthcoming).

Index

Access to financial services, 134–35, 137–38, 139
Afghanistan, 175
Bagehot, Walter, 24, 25–26
Bahamas, 174, 175
Baliño, Tomás J., 98
Banking services: access for underserved populations, 134–35, 137–38, 139; capital mobilization, 26; credit-allocating function, 17, 19–20; DEPTH as measure of, 18–19; economies of scale in, 173–77; expertise for staffing, 175–76; foreign ownership, 174, 176–77; Indonesian liberalization experience, 53, 55–57; insolvent institutions, 40, 41; international assistance, 41–42; lending behaviors, 40, 111, 112; obstacles to assessment, 110–11; offshore intermediaries, 131; opposition to reform in, 63; as prerequisite for economic progress, 127–28; reform crises originating in, 39–40; regulation and supervision. *See* Banking regulation; Prudential regulation; in rural areas, 135; sequencing, 12–13
Bank regulation: avoidance in nonbank institutions, 128, 129–33; balanced, 132–33; Basel Committee recommendations, 110, 130, 139; capital adequacy, 110, 117, 130–31, 140–41, 181–82, 183; central bank independence, 64; competitive neutrality in, 130, 133, 141; crisis intervention, 41; defending against currency speculation, 180; deposit insurance, 113, 114; deposit

insurance alternatives, 116–17; encouraging loan diversification, 183; entry requirements for franchises, 119–20; failures of, 40; as financial repression, 129–30; free banking system, 120; goals, 109–110, 121; incentive compatible, 109; incentive system effects, 112–13; initial conditions as outcome factor, 111–12; interest rate effects, 34, 121–22; intermediation effects, 120; legal system for, 11, 64; monetary policy reform and, 48, 49; narrow banking model, 110, 118–19; for nonbank institutions, 129, 139–41; OECD model, 110, 115–16; political context, 114–15; portfolio concentration, 120–21; rationale, 113–14, 122, 128; regulator skills, 114, 115; relative to market liberalization, 9; requirement for foreign investment, 121; responsiveness of system, 133; shareholder liability limits, 117–18; unregulated parallel markets, 131–32. *See also* Prudential regulation
Barbados, 177
Basel Convention, 110, 130, 139
Bencivenga, Valerie R., 24, 27
Brazil, 151
Brock, Philip L., 27
Calomiris, Charles W., 118
Capital account liberalization, 38–39; sequencing, 39, 47–48
Capital allocation: bank asset requirements, 110, 117, 130–31; banking system assessment, 111;

188